Cneckmate!
The Love Story
of Mikhail Tal and Sally Landau

Sally Landau

Checkmate! The Love Story of Mikhail Tal and Sally Landau
Author: Sally Landau
Translated from the Russian by Ilan Rubin
Typesetting by Andrei Elkov (www.elkov.ru)

© LLC Elk and Ruby Publishing House, 2019 (English version, including corrections and additions to the original Russian edition). All rights reserved
First published in Russia in 1998
Front cover: Sally and Misha the day they announced their engagement
Back cover: Sally and her two husbands, Joe and Misha, Brussels, 1986
Photos provided by the Tal family

Follow us on Twitter: @ilan_ruby
www.elkandruby.com
ISBN 978-5-6041769-6-2

CONTENTS

FOREWORD

Do you want to know how Tal wins?
It's very simple: he places the pieces in the center
and then sacrifices them somewhere
David Bronstein[1]

It is not the purpose of my memoir to recreate the image of Mikhail Tal in its entirety. Nor do I portray him with a saintly halo or as pure and innocent. That is impossible, not least because he was so unusual and ultimately indecipherable.

I am sure that every person who knew him has his own Misha, and that each protects his Misha from denigration by others who think their own opinion to be the ultimate truth. For Gelya, who was his faithful wife and devoted companion during the last 20 years of his life, there is only *her* Misha. For their daughter Zhannochka there is but *her* Misha, *her* father. For Misha's friends, including Alik Bakh, Zhenya Bebchuk, Ratko Knezevic and many others, there exists only their Misha.

For me, Misha will always remain *mine*. My first husband, my first amazing friend, the father of our son Gera, who bears his magic surname *Tal*. This is a memoir of my relations with Misha, encompassing our extraordinary but challenging life together and continuing inexplicably even today. A memoir of our relations at first intimate, then as a family, tender and yet contradictory. Bright moments in our life and sad moments, too. Relations constantly colored by the rainbow of Mikhail Tal's deep, complex, candid yet mysterious personality.

---

[1]   Alexander Koblencs: *Along the Roads of Chess Battles ("Dorogami shakhmatnikh srazhenii")* p. 59 (1963)

This is *my* memoir and this is *Gera's* memoir.

Actually, I am not a writer and would never have written this memoir were it not for one reason: Misha asked me to write it. He did so the very last time we met, in Paris in 1991. He asked me to write about how much he loved me, and would always love me, after he died.

As a result, I had a burning desire to write down on paper my kaleidoscope of memories permeated by my feminine emotions, as well as Gera's memories as a son, so that they may be read by anybody whether or not they know how to play chess.

Sally Landau, Antwerp, 1998

CHAPTER 1

Sally (Saska, Ginger, Sally Landau, Mother of Gera Tal)

Recently I have been increasingly drawn to the conclusion that a person's entire life is just a fleeting moment that somebody has artificially drawn out over a number of years — longer for some than for others — filled with concrete episodes that remain in the "warehouse" of our memory. And we are the keepers of these warehouses. Some warehousemen keep the information in order: "catalogues" of random or planned events, images of people whom you encountered in your life, their portraits, characters, habits, thoughts, expressions, actions. Their names kept in strict alphabetical order. With perfectly recorded chronology. In other words, you have a powerful computer that prints the required text at your command.

But other warehousemen are in charge of a complete mess, a huge mound of unsorted rubbish, rummaging in which you might come across a random detail that reminds you of something that was perhaps not very pleasant, and then you throw it back onto the rubbish tip. Or perhaps it's the opposite — this detail, even if it's just a shred of information, twangs a string deep in your soul, and that string rings out, reviving some old and long forgotten melody, a melody that draws you into a sweet vortex of a unique thrill that you experienced many years earlier. Like old photos or an amateur video, where you captured somebody or somebody captured you. Like a pleasant dream that you don't want to end, that you want to last forever (sometimes, I even naively hope that death will be a languid, gentle eternal dream).

I belong to the second type of "warehousemen". I am an inconsistent and impulsive person, who first does and only then thinks about what I have done. I am an ordinary, vulnerable woman, in which a womanly nature lived and lives, found joy and finds joy, suffered and suffers, in the full sense of those words. The way I see it, selfishness and a desire for independence somehow manage to coexist inside me with love for the people surrounding me and a subconscious wish to be a woman protected by a man who lives for me – protected by him from all sorts of major and minor everyday troubles.

I will be candid in this book. Misha will forgive me. Just as he always forgave me. Because he loved me – well, I'm going to believe so, anyway.

I want to say sorry in advance to those people I neglect to mention when I talk about Misha's friends. Like I said, I'm the second type of warehouseman of memory, all the more so as, following Misha's death, a huge number of people suddenly claimed to have been his "friend". Well, believe me – while Misha was alive most of them didn't even have the right to claim to know him much. But that often happens – after the death of a celebrity the latter suddenly acquires friends, classmates, distant relatives. Just like Mayakovsky and Vysotsky. I say, let's forgive people this weakness, it seems to be a subconscious – or even conscious – desire to increase their importance for the rest of their life.

I also want to apologize in advance for deliberately omitting certain people's names. I just don't want to make them or their families uncomfortable, and far less to outright embarrass them. Maybe they didn't do any wrong to Misha, but, as they say, better safe than sorry. If you recognize those names, then fine, and if you don't, then it's probably for the best: sometimes we should let sleeping dogs lie.

But I want to make clear: I will not hide anything about my life. Really, there is nothing about it to hide. Not even my age. Actually, I'm always a little amused at women who hide their age. It's fine when you're young to add or subtract a few years depending on the circumstances – harmless, purely feminine tricks. But when you're older?!

I can tell you loud and proud: I was born in Vitebsk, in Soviet Belorussia, in 1938. And so that nobody is subsequently disappointed, I'll say right now that my parents were Jewish actors. My father's surname, Landau, which I bear today, is all I have in common with the famous physicist Lev Davidovich Landau, even though many people were convinced that I came from that same family. Well, that mistake is easy to understand: members of ethnic minorities like to believe that they are unusual – if the great Mikhail Tal married Sally Landau, then surely Sally would have been the daughter, or, at worst, the niece of that learned man! Alas, Mikhail Tal married the daughter of two little-known actors.

My mother performed on stage from the age of 13. I don't want to exaggerate – this was not the result of any precocious talent, although as I later discovered she was a good actress. Mother's early professional steps were down to purely worldly circumstances: she had five siblings in the family and they had nothing to eat, so she had to earn money to survive. She won a place at the theatrical institute in Minsk, which is where she met my dad.

My father had quite a remarkable personality. Not to mention his intelligence, acting skills, wicked and yet unusual sense of humor. Misha, I'm pleased to report, adored him. Dad was also a highly talented musician. He could play seven instruments. He was a fantastic light baritone. He was a qualified conductor. Once, Solomon Mikhoels noticed my father on stage. He showered him with praise and, if I'm not mistaken, even invited my father to join his theater. But, as they say, man plans and God laughs. The War with Germany began and it impacted not only my parents' lives...

I was two-and-a-half when Germany invaded, and so I don't remember very much. However, my parents told me that when war broke out I was staying with my grandmother in Vitebsk. The theater where my parents worked would tour throughout the Soviet Union, and when that happened they sent me to grandmother's. The fascist army got so close that my grandmother and my two aunts were forced to literally drop everything and evacuate to Siberia. I have vague memories of a hot, crammed train. And bombings, during which, due to my age, I felt no danger and couldn't understand why my grandmother would smother my body with hers as soon as aircraft appeared in the sky.

One thing I've noticed is that people tend to remember smells from childhood – even now, I associate the word "war" with the smell of boiled eggs and my grandmother's unique fragrance.

Mum and Dad lost us at that point. I later learnt that this was not unusual for that moment in time. The War had broken out in the summer. Many people lost track of their children, brothers and sisters. Many didn't manage to find them even after the War ended. As I said, my memories of those days are vague. And as I mostly lived with my grandmother I actually thought that she was my mother! Grandmother would often say: "Look Sallynka, Mum and Dad will turn up soon." For me that was like an empty sound, an abstract notion. I would ask in reply: "Do I have a second mother?" Grandmother attempted to explain, but I didn't understand.

A few fragments from our Siberian evacuation remain etched in my memory: very kind people, a constant hungry feeling and the whitest of snow under an ardent sun – so much that my eyes watered. Oh, and I clearly remember that people would come to our home, grandmother would plant me on a stool and I would sing. I would sing the patriotic Russian songs Katyusha and Zemlyanka. Of course, I didn't understand their significance, but I sang them anyway. I had a funny little voice (that's what my parents and grandmother told me later), as well as a perfect pitch. Well, people didn't come to our home empty-handed. Some brought milk, others brought eggs. Basically, I was earning my keep through performances from the age of about two-and-a-half.

It then transpired that my parents had turned up in Tashkent, and the Red Cross later found us for them. My Aunty Riva, who was only 13 years older than me, came for me and took me to Tashkent. By that time I was already five years old and it was as though I now met my parents for the first time. I spent a long time calling them "Vy" after that.[2]

To feed themselves, my parents gave illegal concerts on the side and took me with them. At those concerts, I was already singing, accompanied by an orchestra. Basically, I had transformed into a child prodigy. Everybody said that I had a wonderful voice with a range of two octaves. And there was nothing I enjoyed more. Of course, everything is relative – one of my most persistent memories of childhood during the War remains that of constant hunger.

Then I began to sing on the radio, accompanied by my aunt. It was she who insisted that I join the Tashkent music school at the age of six.

---

[2] The formal form of "you" in Russian, rather than the familiar form "ty" which is the equivalent of "thou" in old English (like "vous" and "tu" in French). Normally, a child addresses a parent as "ty" in Russian

It's not for nothing that I'm describing those years in detail: my intense love of the stage, music, singing and the enchanting career of an actress became a permanent leitmotif throughout my life. This was to have a powerful and yet mixed impact on my relationship with Misha.

I only studied for two years in music school, as my parents left with their theater for another town, I can't remember which one but somewhere in central Russia. So I was sent back to stay with my grandmother in Belorussia, but this time in the city of Mogilev, where I was to live for several years. Then, in 1952, all the Jewish theater troupes were abolished. Many leading actors were jailed, some were even shot. Others were confined to mental homes. It was an awful time. My father hid, they came searching for him... Eventually, my parents lucked out: my aunt married a man living in Vilnius in Soviet Lithuania and she helped us to migrate to that city. For my parents, Vilnius was their savior. For me, it became my second home.

I joined the children's music school adjoined to the Vilnius conservatory. So I had to study in two schools simultaneously – in an ordinary school and the music school. It was a huge challenge, given my lack of prowess in maths, chemistry and physics. However, the school would move me from class to class, because I kept winning first prizes in talent competitions. I completed my last two years of secondary education at evening school, but even its modest demands didn't save me – I failed algebra in my end of school exams and my school leaving certificate was held back until the autumn retesting session. Actually, I wasn't particularly bothered by all that, as I was fully focused on music and acting. Clearly, acting was in my genes, and I started to attend a drama club at the conservatory – where my talents soon got noticed.

That was the same summer when I failed my algebra exam, and when the director of the Moscow Art Theater School Radomyslensky visited Vilnius. He noticed me in an amateur drama club production and advised me to drop everything and move to Moscow to study. It wasn't that hard to convince me – I was (and remain) easy to encourage, with a habit for diving into things headlong and with a high opinion of my abilities.

Well, that year turned out to be really lucky for me. Everything worked out great first time around. I got to Moscow and passed the entrance exams in acting for courses in four higher education institutions at once – the Gerasimov Institute of Cinematography, the Moscow Art Theater School, the Russian Institute of Theater Arts and the Vakhtanov School! After that, I was still due to take the entrance exams in ordinary school subjects, although this requirement was just a formality and no particular result was needed. However, the institutions then discovered that I didn't have my school leaving certificate, which was a requirement for being admitted to the entrance exams in ordinary subjects. I told them that I would bring or send them my leaving certificate in the autumn after retaking algebra. Then I returned to Vilnius.

My parents put on a big party for me when I got back, inviting friends and relatives over and telling them the joyful news that their talented little girl had essentially been granted a place at four different Moscow institutions. Everybody was delighted and congratulated me, drinking to my success and eating all the treats that grandmother had cooked. My dad sang and I sang and accompanied myself on the grand piano as well; life looked really rosy.

After that, a conductor from the Vilnius Russian Dramatic Theater, who was amazingly talented but had the rather difficult to remember surname Golovchiner, heard about me and asked

my father to come and meet him at his theater. He said to my
father: "OK, Sallynka goes to Moscow. Think about it. She'll
study there for five long years. And what for? So she can hope to
play Ophelia at the age of 45? Let me suggest a better alternative:
she doesn't have an acting degree but she has talent. I have
actors with degrees from Moscow who don't know how to take
two steps on stage. Let her join my troupe without her degree for
a six-month trial and we shall see."

So seriously, I had all the luck that summer – I joined the
Vilnius Russian Dramatic Theater. Three months later, I was on
stage playing the leading role in a show called Petrarchan Sonnet.
Sally Landau gained the attention of the Vilnius press. Even
now, I look at the newspapers with glowing tributes from time to
time, rereading them with a grin. Well, with a sad grin, actually.
And I say to myself: "I wonder what would have happened if I
had nevertheless gone to study in Moscow? How many talented
and pretty young provincial ladies tried to win over the capital's
theatrical world? And how many of those remained in the role
of reserve understudy to actors who themselves merely dressed
up as mushrooms on stage?"

So I answer myself as follows: "Sally, no matter how trivial it
may sound, fate accorded you a different role. It allocated you
to another theater, where the lead role was played by a Genius,
and where you played the role of his wife. And it's a darned
difficult role to take on – that of a loving and suffering woman,
of a jealous woman and one who caused jealousy in others, a
mother, a sister and a mistress all in one, the role of a dependent
woman striving for independence. Evidently, that role was too
much for you. Yet you were to remain in that role your entire
life, even after the Genius had left the stage."

I was just seventeen.

I met Misha three years later.

I don't wish to burden the reader with events from my acting career at the Vilnius Russian Dramatic Theater. I don't think that was interesting for anybody except for me.

Today, many years later, I come to the conclusion that the story of my life was planned somewhere *over there*. Sometimes, my story crossed that of random people who haven't stuck in my memory – not even their names. At other times, I met people who left a great impression. Be that as it may, my life evolved so that the lead actor would appear front stage. A chain of random events that leads to a logical outcome is something that, as a rule, we only notice afterwards. At the same time, I resembled a sort of fidgety dragonfly, the summer with its red sky seemed to be eternal, and winter would never arrive. I had no ability to predict the future (thank God!). But I possessed other qualities – I sang well, I was talented on the piano, and I was darned pretty. Well, that's what everybody told me, much to my sincere surprise. I couldn't walk the streets without being gawped at. Probably because I was a fiery red-head.

I remember being with Misha at the candidates tournament at Curacao in 1962. Once, we were heading back to the hotel. He stopped, looked at me intensely and, totally seriously, without any irony (which was quite unusual for him!) exclaimed: "Only aliens have hair like that!" My hair isn't just ginger – it's the color of gold nuggets. But the most amazing thing is that my eyes are exactly the same color. Once, during a theater tour in Belorussia, I went into a shop and the sales girl looked at me and went: "Wow, how do you manage to dye your hair to match your eyes?"

Whatever.

The theater leadership decide to perform the play Aesop, and Georgy Baryshnikov from the Vakhtanov Theater was invited to direct it. Once, after a rehearsal, I stepped outside into the building's grounds. It was warm and sunny. I screwed up my eyes tightly and raised my face to the sun. Then I suddenly heard: "Aren't you afraid that your hair will catch fire?"

It was Baryshnikov. He was staring at me so vividly that I felt uncomfortable. I already knew what those stares were about. Yet this time, everything seemed so pure and innocent that I didn't even want to tell him to get lost, though usually I had no trouble expressing myself in similar circumstances.

"Now I understand why they call you Sulamith in Vilnius," he continued.

Handsome men never had a chance to become the hero of my love story. Not then, not ever. I didn't care for handsome men. Baryshnikov was no exception to my preferences: a fantastic intellect, erudition and fantastic tact. He was fairly short, a bit podgy and wore glasses. He was 32 to my 18. Well, I shan't bore you with the details – he became my first man and my teacher in everything: theater, life, love. Our relationship bloomed so rapidly that he left his wife and we agreed that he would take me to Moscow, to the Vakhtanov Theater. Aesop's run ended and I saw Baryshnikov off at Vilnius airport. I can still see his face in the window of that little aircraft. I didn't have any bad premonitions. No, I was full of joy at what I expected the future to bring.

Two days later, his mother called me from Moscow to tell me that Georgy had died of a heart attack. So fate had now twice held me back from moving to Moscow. If I wanted to dress things up I could have invented a story that some random gypsy had predicted that I would soon engage on a fairly short journey to another city. But there was no gypsy. Just frustration, drawn-out depression and a feeling of disgust for the theater and for everything that reminded me of Georgy.

Well, it so happened that at that time the Riga Youth Theater came on tour, and its director, Pavel Khomsky, offered me the chance to join it as an actress, meaning I would thereby move to Riga. My will at that time was so paralyzed and my apathy so pronounced that had he suggested I move to Tallinn, Bryansk, Novosibirsk or anywhere else I would have agreed just as easily. I just couldn't bear to remain in Vilnius, even though I liked and still like that beautiful city. I would have surely hanged myself from sadness and loneliness. Neither my parents nor my grandmother could have helped me. Pasha Khomsky turned out to be the last-grasp straw that saved me at the time, and the vector of my fate underwent an abrupt change.

So I moved to Riga, became an actress at the Riga Youth Theater, and devoted myself entirely to my job: to rehearsals, shows and concerts. I should point out that the theater and social lives in Riga were more intense than in Vilnius, more appropriate for a capital city. Apart from the theater performances, I began to take part in concerts as a variety singer. The public apparently began to come to the concerts especially to hear me. Fans appeared and I would sign autographs. I had all sorts of offers, both professional and personal – there were even some famous men who wanted to marry me. But I didn't want to think about that! My head was full of singing and acting. Added to that, I'd fallen in love with Khomsky. Oh, I was lucky in life with talented men. But I also grew attached to Khomsky like a little homeless dog. Sensitive and tactful, he drew me out of my depression and became a true friend, rather than some director exploiting his subordinates, as sometimes happens. So there could be no marriage to discuss. Anyway, I would have considered marriage as losing my independence and my opportunity to do a job I loved.

Still, sharp contradictions coexisted within me: on the one hand, this immense fear of losing my personal freedom, on the other hand, this equally immense fear of solitude and a subconscious desire to have a strong man beside me with whom I wouldn't be afraid of falling off an overturned boat in the open seas, even if I didn't know how to swim. These contradictions played a significant role in my life with Misha...

There were a number of places in Riga frequented by the elite – an ethnically mixed set of actors, sportsmen, doctors, lawyers and so on. And while racial background remained a sensitive subject, we all got on great – ethnic Latvians, Russians and Jews. There was something quite European in this Riga air – in a most positive way. Or maybe it only seemed like that to us, because the real Europe was something we had only heard about. Or seen on TV.

My friends at the time included a young doctor called Sasha Zamchuk. Now, he's a renowned urologist in Moscow. In late December 1958, Sasha invited me to see in the New Year in the famous Riga restaurant Astoria. In those days, it was a trendy hang-out with exquisite service, fantastic cuisine and a fun head waiter called Robert, who was a legend throughout the city.

And so it came to pass that on New Year's Eve in 1958 Sasha Zamchuk introduced me in the Astoria to his old classmate with whom he had sat at the same desk in school, the by now famous Misha Tal. In fact, that's how Sasha introduced him: "I'd like you to meet the famous Misha Tal!"

I had heard a couple of times that there was a young and supremely talented chess player called Tal, but I couldn't have cared less. Firstly, I had absolutely zero interest in chess, and, secondly, there were lots of celebrities around. Moreover, that New Year's Eve, Tal made no impression on me whatsoever, so I was totally indifferent to the impression I made on him. Then,

Sasha invited me to dance and spent the whole dance elaborating just what a genius Misha was, how unique he was, and how he was going to become a world champion. Meanwhile, an endless flow of people kept coming up to Misha, introducing themselves or introducing other people, and they constantly invited him to sit at their tables. Then, people started to split into groups and we, a group of actors, left for Dubulti in Jurmala, where we ended our New Year celebrations at the villa of a popular Rigan artist.

...When little Misha started school he was immediately moved up to the third year – that's how gifted he was. He was just 15 when he graduated from school and was admitted to Riga University. Well, 20-year old Komsomolets[3] Mikhail is now in his fifth and final year in the history and languages faculty.

...It's now been several years since we first heard that there was a young chap in Riga who plays great chess, quickly, almost without thinking, calculating the most intricate variations.

...At the start of the 24th USSR championship A. Kotov claimed "Tal will come first!" His view was an isolated one. Even Tal himself didn't believe him.

...Given the modern development of chess, especially in our country, it's very hard to achieve such huge success. To play a marathon 21 rounds, to emerge virtually unscathed from the crucible of eight international grandmasters, and to outperform them – that's an amazing achievement in our game! It's hard, almost impossible in our championships to gain grandmaster norms.

---

[3]   A member of the communist youth organization. Membership didn't however signify that the member was a committed communist

GMs don't like it when their "family" grows in size. They are the strictest of examiners. Well, this time it was the young player who turned out to be the examiner. Although Tal is still young, it's clear that in him the chess family has gained a totally mature top-class GM.

...In 1935, the young USSR champion Mikhail Botvinnik became the first Soviet GM. Many years later, Botvinnik became world champion. Today, Mikhail Tal has become Soviet GM number 19. Maybe these two Mikhails will one day meet in a match!

Salo Flohr, *Ogoniok*[4], 1957

Four decades have elapsed since that New Year's Eve. Misha is no longer with us. But I have the constant feeling that he has simply gone off somewhere from where he can't easily phone. I communicate with him in my dreams, which I have frequently. They are quite realistic dreams, and if some phone call from Moscow, Paris or Berlin wakes me from my dreams in the morning (I now live in Antwerp, Belgium) I grab the receiver with excitement: at last Misha is calling me! But then I get shaken up when it's not his voice and I become aware of reality – it's not him, and he will never call me again. Never, never, never...

Since childhood, I have always been afraid of this cold-sounding word "never". I remember from time to time asking my grandmother: "If I die will we never see each other again?" She would exclaim something back in Yiddish. I didn't understand what she was saying but by intonation I guessed it was something like: "God, tell this little urchin to stop uttering such nonsense!" But I gradually become more insistent and

---

[4]   A current and social affairs magazine

wouldn't stop. Then grandmother answered: "Never! Never! And I don't want to hear this ever again!" But that wasn't enough for me: "And tomorrow 'never'? And the day after 'never'? And the day after that? And in a million years' time? But surely 'someday' will occur?" It seemed to me that in a million years' time this "never" would end, and the dead me would suddenly open her eyes and again see grandmother, I would see the sun, because this "never" had ended. But almost immediately, a nasty cold feeling ran through my body and I realized that this "never" would be eternal.

I was convinced that Misha couldn't disappear from my life. Whatever happened to him, no matter how hopeless a situation he might find himself in, no matter how pessimistic the doctors' prognoses, I was sure that he would pull through – that was his character – and he would live eternally with all of his ailments.

I think about that New Year's Eve and everything that happened after that throughout my life, and sometimes it seems to me that it wasn't that night that Misha first appeared in my life, that it happened much earlier, that he was even listening as I sang Zemlyanka to our guests while standing on the stool in that Siberian village during the War. He was among those people. As though somebody had drawn us together using magnetism. And I could never "get rid" of him forever, just as he could never "get rid" of me.

Several days after the New Year party, Sasha Zamchuk phoned and asked if I had liked Tal. I replied that I was indifferent. So what if he's Tal? "Well, he certainly liked you," Sasha told me. Of course, I was pleased to hear that. Never believe a woman who tells you she doesn't care whether or not men like her. Then, a couple of days later, our administrator in the theater, Grigory Efimovich, approached me to say: "Sallynka, people saw you sitting at the same table as Misha Tal at New Year. You really should get to know him better. The boy's a genius and from a really good family."

Then, after my friend in Riga told me shortly after that she wanted to invite me to the home of her friend Misha Tal, who was dying to welcome me there, I realized that I was "under siege", and I became curious.

So that's how one evening I found myself in the Tals' home for the first time. I remember being immediately awe struck at the apartment. It wasn't the amazingly beautiful antique furniture or the fantastic crystal chandelier hanging over the large, heavy, imposing table. I have never been impressed by worldly goods, even though I believe I am a good judge of beauty. I never cared for expensive jewelry. Misha always said that I was indifferent to money.

I remember that when we lived in Tashkent my parents once sent me to get bread, to "monetize" our ration cards as they would say. But an old beggar woman approached me and I gave her all my cards. Just imagine the scandal that my parents raised when I got back home – we were going to be left without bread until the end of the month. However, it turned out that the old woman had surreptitiously followed me all the way home. She knocked on the door and gave the cards back to my parents. So they fed her, put some clothes on her and, before she left, she said the nicest thing I ever heard in my direction: "Little girl, I will pray for you all my life."

So it wasn't the external appearance of the Tals' apartment that struck me that evening. Rather, it was its anti-Soviet spirit that I sensed. I immediately inhaled this pleasant middle-class air. Anybody who has been in that apartment understands what I mean. It was apparent straight away that the people living there were not "mass-produced" but very much "hand-crafted", and that relations between them did not fit into the usual framework of socialist society.

I was met my Ida, Misha's mother, the elegant Robert, Misha's father, and Misha himself. He was agitated and somewhat nervous.

This time, I took a more detailed look at him. He was short and a bit puny. Huge eyes which seemed to reflect constantly changing mischievous thoughts and ideas, wonderfully curved eyebrows, a pronounced nose and a unique lower rubber lip which he loved to stick out.

The conversation didn't seem to take off. We were all somewhat shy. As one does, they showed me around their apartment and I noticed the portrait of an attractive-looking man hanging on the wall. "Who is it?" I asked. "That's my father," replied Misha, "Doctor Tal."

It was only much later that I discovered that Misha's biological father was actually Robert, while Doctor Tal was officially his father. That's a story in itself, underlining the unusual relations within the Tal family. I will return to it later.

Then Misha said suddenly: "I heard from Sasha Zamchuk that you are a great singer. We have a piano, please sing something."

These days, I'm quite shy about playing the piano or singing, and it's rare for somebody to convince me to do so. But in those days, you didn't have to beg me at all. I could sing or play music for hours on end no matter where I was.

I sat down and played my favorite Elegie by Rachmaninoff. I was subsequently to play it countless times at Misha's request! He adored Rachmaninoff, whose music was precisely in tune with Misha's mood.

I also recall Misha's look of surprise when he suddenly heard this young, pretty red-head playing Rachmaninoff. He gazed at

me as though he had made an amazing discovery. I then sang
another song which was to become a sort of "secret code" in my
relations with Misha, a popular song at the time entitled "I have
told you not all the words":

I have told you not all the words
On the way I lost them.
I have told you not the right words
It's so hard to find them.

All sorts of things happened between us when we lived
together, and after we stopped living together, but my phone
could suddenly ring and from somewhere in Buenos Aires or
Rio-de-Janeiro I would be sure to hear *I have told you not all the*
words sung to me. Well, I really do think that he didn't say all the
words to me in our life, and, sadly, I didn't manage to say all the
words to him, either.

I suppose I sang and played the piano pretty well. At least,
Misha often said so when he introduced me to his friends: "This
is my wife. If there are 13 dudes at our gathering then 12 will fall
in love with her straight away and the thirteenth will fall for her
as soon as she sits down to play the piano and sing."

After my friend and I got up to leave, Misha told me that he
was heading to Tbilisi for the USSR championships (9 January –
11 February 1959), asked for my phone number and wondered
whether I would mind if he called me from there. I said that I
wouldn't mind. However, I didn't expect his innocent *would I*
mind to transform into a bombardment of calls every day.

Meanwhile, I was obsessed with Khomsky. Sometimes, I
imagine myself as a sort of tool capable of capturing the impulses
of talent, or, at least, of uniqueness. The sacred flame of talent
could sometimes light a fire inside me that would continue to
burn for as long as I threw the firewood of my imagination onto
it. I had the habit of endowing people in my mind with the

qualities that I wanted to see them possess. People like me often become the victims of deception, or are at least disappointed. In this respect, though, God amnestied me. Not always, of course, but these things didn't happen to me too often.

The Pasha Khomsky with whom I fell in love was hence pretty much a product of my imagination. Our relationship had sprung out of nowhere, but it didn't last long, which was fortunate for both of us.

Our relationship in fact peaked just when Misha bombarded me with calls from Tbilisi. Maybe those "attacks" played a role in ending it. At the very least, when he returned from Riga my fantasies about Pasha ran dry and the fire inside me was extinguished just as suddenly as it had been ignited.

So Misha and I began to see each other. Excuse me for using this word "see". I can't stand this euphemism and I'm using the word "see" here in its more literal sense. Misha often invited me to his home, where I would be welcomed by his mother and Robert. They were exceptional people, extremely smart and tactful. Talking to them gave me great pleasure, but it was not always easy. The problem was that Rigan celebrity life could not ignore a young, pretty and by now popular actress without trapping her in a web of absurd stories, false and sometimes disgusting rumors. They said that I had driven the talented theater director Baryshnikov to his death, that I had attempted to destroy Khomsky's family. They said I was immoral because of the risque role that I had played in a show called The Devil's Windmill. And God knows what else. So it was understandable that the entire Tal clan was worried about Misha and became rather wary of me. I felt it even though neither Ida, nor Robert, nor Misha's brother Yasha (Yakov) gave me any reason to suspect such in either their visual expressions or words.

Misha and I only broached such a delicate subject once. His interest in me, his courting of me, had grown exponentially. He wasn't giving me any space to breathe. He would meet me at the actors' entrance after each show ended. Robert had a Pobeda car at the time and Misha would make Robert drive him on show days to the theater. They would then wait for a considerable time in the car until I appeared and then "kidnap" me. Robert wasn't enamored with this "work", but he did it to please Misha, whose every word was a command for him. Well, after one such "kidnapping" I asked Misha whether his reputation would suffer from spending time with such a dissolute personality (in the minds of Rigan high society) as me. He looked at me with his typical Tal-like ironically surprised face but said nothing. Yet the meaning of his look was clear: "You misjudge me."

So that's how we dated. We found each other fun. We could talk about any subject. Misha was perfectly educated and very erudite. All his opinions were expressed intelligently and subtly, with a desire to make his conversation partner enjoy the discussion, and, I'm sure, so that he too could enjoy it. I don't remember him ever saying anything rude or allowing a double-entendre. And if anybody drew him into a conversation on a delicate subject, Tal would maintain the discussion on the level of a brilliant French diplomat.

I started to think that our relations would remain on this friendly, platonic level, that neither of us were much interested in the other aspects of a relationship. But of course that isn't something that happens in life if you're talking about two normal healthy individuals, rather than intellectual freaks. His brother Yasha, a divorcee without children, rented an apartment at the time so he lived in a different block. Once, after a high society party, Misha and I found ourselves back at Yasha's apartment.

His brother was travelling somewhere, and that's when our relationship ceased to be platonic.

Misha certainly wasn't shy, but nor was he a "ladies' man". He was a clean-looking young fellow, almost like a little boy. Well, he was only 22. So what about me? Was I really only twenty?

It was wonderful! That night, and the following ones. Describing physical intimacy in words is a pointless and hopeless task. It's a mystery. It's fine to describe if only one of he or she understands it. But if the mystery is revealed to both of them at once then this intimacy becomes a pleasure that cannot be described in words, painted on canvas or expressed in the most exquisite combination of musical notes. And that's how it was with Misha.

Those nights changed many things, simplified some but complicated others...

After those nights, Misha ceased to be a mere "friend". We now sensed that inexplicable feeling of belonging to one another. When people are sincere they experience that feeling after the first time they become intimate. Some feel an inferiority complex leading to dependency, others have a superiority complex, while much less often (unfortunately!) others still feel they are equals in the relationship. Only in that third case the cynically-sounding, cold, industrial term "making love" becomes something different – a natural need for both of them. I immediately felt that Misha was "mine". Not in the sense of possessing him, but like a blood relative or a kindred spirit. No ownership claims on each other, no restrictions, no abnormal requests and, heaven forbid, no ridiculous demands.

At the time, I didn't have the faintest thought of marrying Misha. Still, I felt genuine spiritual comfort, and everything involving my relations with Misha gave me pleasure and joy:

whenever we met, whenever he gifted me flowers with an ironic expression, and everything that could happen after. In those days, flowers were all that he bought me, though Misha was no scrooge throughout our life together. He was so tactful and gentlemanly that from his point of view more expensive presents would have been somewhat humiliating for me, demonstrating that I was dependent on him. Misha hated such "tricks", whether in everyday life or on the chess board. He never gained any pleasure from winning games due to an opponent's blunder.

In fact, it seems to me that Tal, especially when he was young, was convinced that he was born to win, to win beautifully and comprehensively. "I'll smash him to smithereens," he frequently said to me before games. He considered all of his wins to be the sole logical outcome: how could any other result occur? And plainly he viewed me as his conquest, one that he had achieved in a fair battle, one that he had dreamed of and which brought him huge joy. And now this victory had to belong to him, because only he knew the taste of victory, because he was Tal, because any other outcome was unimaginable.

...We love Tal for his uniquely quick-witted, lively, joyful way of playing, for his devotion to chess beauty, for his incessant search for original moves, for stunning sacrifices, for improvising, for risk...

...Maintaining the traditions of Morphy, Chigorin, Yanofsky and Spielmann, he has added an important and brutal detail to their chess philosophy – a crystal clear understanding of the inevitability of chess chaos and that it is practically impossible for a living person to calculate even approximately the consequences of the upcoming moves.

This understanding of the direction of the battle allows Tal to calculate variations with legendary speed and to see that the

*position he is creating cannot be solved at the board. And he...
simply tries to take in as much of the position as possible in the
minimum amount of time! Meanwhile, his opponent, whom he
has craftily dragged into this whirlwind of complications, tries to
calculate everything to the end. Naturally, this gets him nowhere.
Then, Tal's opponent starts to get nervous, panics and selects what
superficially appears to be the simplest line, as a result of which
he imperceptibly edges over a cliff. Tal scored win after win in his
early days in particular, yet even today this side of his play hasn't
been properly understood.*

David Bronstein, *64*, 1969

Well, I didn't consider myself defeated. I was the same Sally
Landau – independent, proud and popular. I remained the
same person with the one difference that I now had a very close
man who above all understood *me*. That is what was important
to me, and not the fact that he was a brilliant chess player and
expected to become the next world champion. He could just
as easily have been an engineer or a musician. I couldn't have
cared less for his social status.

Actually, Misha was the sort of guy who sincerely believed
that if he was hungry I must be starving too. If he simply fancied
wandering around Riga then he was sure that I wanted to as
well. If he was giving a simul to children at a chess club then he
believed that I definitely wanted to watch. This unintended yet
constant pressure began to provoke a feeling of protest inside
me.

"Look, I'm not a doll, you know," I once said to him, unable
to restrain myself any longer.

Misha glanced at me in surprise and answered putting on his
unique disarming smile: "I know that you're not a doll. You're
my Sally."

And a shadow would appear and disappear again: we began to argue. Once he even turned up at the home of my best friend, Inna Mandelstam, and complained that I spent too much time with her.

"Misha!" I exclaimed. "I'm an independent person and spend time with whomever I want. Surely you see that you have no right to kick up a scandal with Inna!"

"I don't have the right," replied Tal. "I apologize to her. But she's taking my Sally from me."

He said sorry. Peace was reestablished. Our belonging to each other turned out to be stronger than our belonging to ourselves. I guess that is the sweet pain of love.

However, we are both Scorpios, and so it's not difficult to imagine what punishment that meted out! We again quarreled – this time, because I didn't want to stay the night with him and wanted to get a proper night's sleep on my own in my own apartment, that's to say in the apartment of Amanda Mikhailovna, my landlady. I was very tired and needed to sleep as I had a morning performance the next day. As that awful argument broke out, his face suddenly became distorted – it was no longer his but became unfamiliar and frightening, as though a Demon had settled in him. He grabbed my arm but then stopped and ran off. Sometime later, after we again patched things up, he could find no logical explanation for his action, for which he was willing to disappear into the Earth's entrails. He said: "If I ever get into that state again just hug and kiss me. Because I obey you more than I obey anybody else."

Later that same 1959, I became his full hostage in this respect. Yet the subject of marriage wasn't broached. At least, I continued to have no such thoughts, and Misha never raised the matter.

We seriously split up about three times in that first year. Each time, I thought it was for good. Once, we were in a restaurant with friends and quarreled so fiercely that Misha got blind drunk on brandy and our friends had great difficulty in persuading the driver to take him home. It was awful. I had never before seen Misha in that state. It was again as though it wasn't Misha, that somebody else had got into his body. I then saw him again a month and a half later, but neither of us brought up the details of that evening. Actually, "Tal plus alcohol" was a favorite theme of both certain thick but extremely uninhibited journalists and some of the people who hung out with us, Misha's so-called friends. That's a story unto itself.

It was difficult being with Misha, and I often wondered: "Sally, what's going on? Where is your independence? He has no right to be suspicious and jealous, to restrict your freedom. So what's this all about? Why do you leave after every scene, convinced that you will never return, and yet sooner or later you are joyful to hear at last his phone call when he says he wants to reconcile with you, and you rush back to him as though nothing has happened?"

And each time I was unable to provide a sensible answer to any of these questions. Evidently, my pride prevented me from admitting that Misha had hurt me. Or perhaps I still didn't realize it. Whatever it was, I was drawn to him, to his look with which he impaled me like a moth on a pin, to his uniqueness, his paradoxical pronouncements, his voice... And not only his voice. And once again, I found myself in a mad idyll of tenderness and passion that would end in an argument just when I least expected it.

For example, one morning after the most tender of nights he suddenly locked the door and said that he wouldn't let me go to my rehearsal, that he didn't want me to work at the theater any more. Once it dawned on me that Misha wasn't joking, I told him in no uncertain terms that if he didn't let me out it really would be the end of our relationship, because nothing was more important to me than my personal freedom and my theatrical work. I said that with such resolve and conviction that he obediently extended his hand to offer me the key and said to me with concern: "Are you serious?" "Absolutely!" I replied, pronouncing the word syllable by syllable.

Then something bizarre happened: he opened the medicine box, grabbed a handful of pills, and said: "If you leave I will swallow all these pills, and if they don't work I'll throw myself out the window." I wrenched the pills from his hand and told him bluntly: "Had this scene taken place in my apartment I would simply have chucked you out." He replied: "Turn on your actress's imagination and imagine that you are in your own apartment!" So I continued: "Then get out and forget my address! I'll leave the key under the mat." So he left. I heard him run down the stairs and slam the door to the street. I looked out the window and saw him stopping the first passing car. Then I left for the theater and told myself that this really was the end. With my personality, it's sometimes difficult for me to tell who is right and who is wrong.

We had a packed rehearsals schedule. We were set to leave to put on a show in Vilnius, and the day of our departure couldn't come soon enough for me. I hoped that time would solve all my problems, all the more so as Tal was due to play at a tournament in Switzerland (Zurich, 19 May - 8 June 1959). My thought process was quite primitive: he would leave for the tournament and I would leave for the show. We would not see each other for a considerable amount of time, if at all, and would gradually forget each other. I would meet somebody else, he would meet somebody else. As doctors say, replacement therapy would do its stuff. The key was to avoid giving the impression of being surplus to his requirements.

Out of the blue, our administrator Grigory Efimovich, who was sort of considered my guardian at the theater, told me on one of those days: "Sallynka, Misha's uncle[5] came here and said that after your last quarrel Misha had a nervous breakdown, he's in some sort of trance, spends all his time lying in bed, refuses to get up, to eat, to sleep. The uncle also said that he doesn't plan to get involved in your relations with Misha, but for the sake of Misha's mother, who is now quite depressed and whom you are so fond of, he begs you to visit Misha and make up with him, so that he can get a grip on himself and go to the tournament in Switzerland."

I listened to Grigory Efimovich and then asked him: "But what do you think?" He replied that if I'm interested in his opinion then I should reconcile with Tal, firstly because it would be madness to lose such a person as Tal, and secondly, because I should not be risking the health and future of a person who was the national pride of Latvia and, probably, of the entire Soviet Union. I remember saying "Grigory Efimovich! I really value your view, and I do really like Misha's mother, but I won't go to him because I've already made up my mind, and seeing as I've made up my mind I don't care about the career of the 'national pride of Latvia'. And if he's ill then they should call a doctor."

To tell the truth, I was just "acting out" the role of this imperious, irreconcilable woman. In reality, I knew that Misha's state was not the whim of a spoilt child, but was a real nervous breakdown of a man used to always doing things his own way

---

[5]   Robert was sometimes known as "Uncle Robert"

and who had suddenly come up against an equally stubborn and capricious creature. I knew that I only had to turn up at his apartment at 34 Gorky Street and everything would be resolved: Misha would smile, his eyes would come alive, and he would immediately try to crack a joke and say something like "God helps those who help themselves," after which the illness would disappear without a trace. Then, he would again become jovial, easy-going, loving and happy. In fact, he would be doubly happy: first, because the girl that he loved would once again be next to him, and second, because this time everything had turned out in true Tal fashion – he had won. Although I'm not sure: maybe this "second" was actually "first" for him.

Anyhow, I was determined to stay away from Gorky Street. If I was fated to spend some sort of future with him he needed to get it into his head that I was no obedient doll but a living person equal to him by all measures, apart from being of a different gender. Oh, we were a textbook example of a pair of Scorpios. Several years later, Misha's mother said to me: "You remind me of two stubborn and disobedient beasts who bite and scratch each other constantly, but as soon as you are parted each curls up in a corner, refuses food and may die from depression." She was a very wise woman, and our subsequent lives proved that she was right.

Many years after Misha and I divorced and each of us had another family, a telepathic wave continued to link us. Sometimes, I woke up in the middle of the night with the feeling that something bad had happened to Misha. I would then be struck down by my monstrous migraine and might even faint. Then, at that moment, the phone would ring from abroad. And I knew that it would be Misha calling. I would hear him sing down the phone "I have told you not all the words," and then I would feel relief.

Now I keep thinking, suppose Misha and I had met not as young creatures, but ten years later, with some life experience behind our backs? Would we have been more compromising in our attitude to each other? Might we have felt this mysterious biological interdependence while avoiding many sorry mistakes that left painful scars in our souls? Probably, yes. Anyway, I don't think that I could have ever evolved into a stereotypical "chess wife". The wives of great chess players, poets and writers are unusual women. Some are themselves great people and others less so, but that's not the point. Rather, they are a special category of people to which I do not belong. Though who knows what would have and wouldn't have happened.

Basically, I left for Vilnius with my troupe several days later, while the doctors nevertheless managed to get Misha on his feet and he did make it to Switzerland. I didn't care whether or not he played well at that tournament. Rather, I did my utmost to erase him from my memory, though my attempts failed and I had this constant feeling of frustration with myself.

One day, we were heading in a bus to a show. One of our actors, Roma Veksler, sat down next to me and said: "You see, Sally, you dumped Tal, as they say, but it doesn't seem to have mattered to him — he took first prize in Switzerland, while for you *happiness was so attainable, so near* [6]."

"Roma!" I replied. "The reason he took first place was because I 'dumped' him, as you put it. He thinks that now he's such a hero I'll realize what a mistake I made. He is a Farlaf [7], like most men! But like most men, he is mistaken!"

---

[6] These words in italics are a quote from Eugene Onegin by Pushkin

[7] A big-headed but cowardly character in Ruslan and Ludmila by Pushkin

"No, Sally," Roma continued, "he is no Farlaf. He's more like Ruslan, who as you know searched for his Ludmila and didn't care for Naina."

Well, that got me going! I told Roma I would bet him anything he wished that I only needed to phone Tal and he would not so much come running as come flying that very second. Actually, I wasn't so sure that that was true, but I got all hot-headed and we made a bet. Without any stakes as such.

Needless to say, my parents were most upset that I'd fallen out with Tal. They really hoped that we would marry, especially my father. Well, imagine their joy when I came to their home after a show and phoned Riga (as Misha had by this time returned from Switzerland).

"Misha," I said in a voice as though nothing had happened between us, "I'm in Vilnius on a tour. Come and visit if you want." And then I put the receiver down. You see, as I mentioned earlier, a chain of random events still leads to a logical outcome. Who could have known that Roma Veksler would provoke me into a schoolkid bet leading to my calling Riga – which would play a critical role in my future, and not only mine?

Much later, I found out that Misha had a girlfriend in Moscow, the well-known piano player Bella Davidovich. Her husband had died, leaving her with a young child. Her relations with Misha gradually evolved into something more than just friendly. Moreover, Misha's parents didn't at all mind if he wanted to marry her. However, my reappearance in Misha's "orbit" against my better judgement pushed that matter way into the distance, if not completely removing it from the agenda.

Our last argument had somehow revived our not completely collapsed relations, all the more so as Misha's parents, as I had already said, really wanted their son to finally grow up, stop womanizing and focus entirely on his chess. That evening, after my phone call from Vilnius, Misha flew into his mother's bedroom and exclaimed: "Murochka!" (that's how Tal called his mother – he always loved to give people silly pet names).[8] "I was planning to go and visit Bella, but Sally just called me. I will do whatever you tell me!"

Misha's mother told me all this a couple of years after I married him. "Darling daughter!" she said to me. "Believe me, no matter how I replied Misha would have left for Vilnius. Therefore, I made do with the evasive reply 'Do what your heart tells you.'"

As you have obviously guessed, I won my now fateful bet with Roma. The very next day, Misha was already in Vilnius. While I, who just the day before had considered myself completely cured of the "Tal syndrome", was extremely glad that he had arrived. It was like a huge weight lifted from my heart.

Tal's arrival in Vilnius caused a double commotion. Firstly, because the "wizard Tal" had come to Vilnius, and secondly, because he had come to visit Sally Landau – the local Vilnius girl!

Misha stayed with us at my parents' home. My parents were delighted – their dream was coming true. Our house was constantly full of guests – some closer to us than others – just to see the chess star and boast the day after: "Yesterday I went to visit the Landaus and Misha Tal was there. We became friends. An amazingly talented boy, and so witty."

Tal, both then and subsequently, was always very friendly and easy-going, and he loved meeting people. He could find a common language with just about any conversation partner, even if that person wasn't particularly interesting. He had

---

[8]   Murochka is usually a pet name for a cat, rather than a person

perfect manners and could never offend anybody by ignoring them or by arrogance. This quality led to many people claiming to be his friend even if they had only met him once. That was the story throughout his life. It has even continued after his death — all sorts of "friends" appear out of nowhere in the press, on the radio and TV and start to talk often the most incredible nonsense about him. It's painful to read and hear but what can I do?

As well as having these guests over, we were invited to all sorts of receptions, soirees and birthday parties. Vilnius was by now brimming with rumors that Tal had asked for Sally Landau's hand in marriage. Well, there was some substance behind those rumors...

At the time, a chess master called Isakas Vistaneckis lived in Vilnius. He was tall, handsome and a real celeb. One day in that now distant 1959, at a reception in Misha's honor, he suddenly got up and proposed raising a glass "to our charming fellow countrywoman Sally Landau, who is getting married to a representative of our fraternal Baltic republic." Everybody jumped to their feet and began to clink glasses with us and proffer their congratulations. The orchestra churned out some ceremonial refrain. I looked in astonishment at Misha, but he just shrugged his shoulders and, sticking out his lower lip, mysteriously stared at the ceiling. Then he leaned towards me, kissed me on the cheek and said quietly: "Vistaneckis is a strong master and is unlikely to have miscalculated." So imagine my situation. What was I to do? Deny it? Get angry? That would have been totally daft! So I accepted the congratulations, thanked the people and laughed it off. I'm sure that Tal used the mouth of Vistaneckis to carry out one of his risky winning combinations. Of course, I should have seen it coming. He sensed that I was delighted he had come to Vilnius and made a move to end the uncertainty in our relations. I can't say that he sacrificed anything for my sake: he did it for himself, too. He wanted this because he loved me and because he was sure that I loved him. It wasn't Vistaneckis who hadn't miscalculated, it was Tal who hadn't miscalculated.

The next morning, I accepted congratulations for the previous evening's "betrothal", which had by then been reported in a local newspaper.

We returned to Riga together, and I decided to leave Amanda Mikhailovna's apartment and move to the theater's hostel, as the apartment was too expensive for me, while I didn't yet have a good justification for moving in with Misha. Moreover, my concept of a future family life involved a separate apartment for just me and Misha. He, on the other hand, couldn't imagine any option other than living on Gorky Street together with Murochka and "Jack" (as Misha called Robert). In that rosy period of our life, it was probably the only source of disagreement between us. We eventually agreed a compromise – I would spend much of my time at the Tal home, often staying the night there, but the suitcase with my belongings remained at the hostel and I nominally lived there.

I guess this is a good time to talk about the Tal family. I've already mentioned the impression that these people and their apartment made on me when I first stepped into their home. I was also struck by the relations between Ida and Robert – an odd mixture of simplicity and subtleness. At first, I was also surprised at relations between Misha and Robert. The portrait of Misha's father Doctor Nekhemia Tal hanging in the apartment surrounded by a halo of love and protection was a mystery to me. Ida didn't immediately admit me to her trove of secrets. She did that gradually and without being pushy as she increasingly began to love me not only as the object of Misha's worship but for who I was, independently of my relations with her son. Right until her death, she remained for me not so much Misha's mother, as much as a unique and most wise woman, my friend, my second mother. Our relations were not changed one bit after Misha and I divorced. Her love for me even today provides support to my self-esteem. I often dream about her. She sits down on the bed, strokes my head and pronounces a sentence which she once said in one of the darker periods of my life: "I don't know why I love you so much... maybe it's because you understand my son..."

When she was young, she had a passionate affair with her first cousin, Nekhemia Tal. Then, fate separated them: Ida left to study art in Berlin, while Nekhemia went to Leningrad to study medicine. She completed her studies, returned to Riga and learnt that Nekhemia Tal had fallen in love with somebody else, so much so that he was planning to marry her. This was a huge shock for her, and in order to dull the pain she went back to Berlin, and from there she moved to Paris. Being highly-educated, with perfect manners and unusually attractive, she blended into Parisian high society, spending time with the likes of Ilya Ehrenburg, Louis Aragon, Elsa Triolet and Pablo Picasso.

She was no longer young when I first met her, yet I was struck by the amazing way that she had retained her youth, with her refined and elegant figure, and those indefinable charms that make a woman a Woman in the most mysterious sense of the word. Add her opulent hair that must have been a challenge for any brush, a sharp, eagle-like nose, completely green eyes, a noble demeanor, her unhurried manner of talking and a totally calm personality (I don't like agitated people!); plus any other qualities that you would expect in a real woman, and you have Ida Tal. The saying "nothing makes a woman age more than growing older" didn't apply to Ida Tal.

After Paris, she returned to Riga and again hooked up with Nekhemia, now known as Dr. Tal. His marriage had never happened. He would recall his passion as simply a fact from his student days. His relations with Ida acquired a quite new quality. They married and loved each other as only wise and tactful people can. They had a son, Yasha, Misha's elder brother.

Yasha was the spitting image of Dr. Tal. I noticed this the first time that I glanced at the portrait hanging on the apartment wall. At the same time, I noted that Misha's features had nothing in common with those of his father in the portrait, whereas he resembled Robert closely. The truth emerged later, when I became a full member of the Tal family, above all in Ida's eyes.

Dr. Tal died a year before I met Misha. Everyone who knew him talked about him like he was a saint. Even his portrait was saintly, as though hanging above everything worldly. He had worked at a special clinic in Riga. Doctors whom I knew informed me that Dr. Tal was the only Jewish doctor at the clinic. It wasn't difficult to understand that situation, given all the nuances of ethnic policy in the Soviet Union in general and Latvia in particular. All the more so, as Riga didn't evade either the witch hunt against "cosmopolitans" or the campaign against "murderers in white overalls" during the notorious "Doctor's Plot". However, Dr. Tal's authority as a physician was so high that nobody dared to touch him.

He was totally respectful towards Ida. It was said that when they went for walks he would hold her hand as though he were carrying a fragile receptacle that he didn't want to drop containing liquid that he didn't want to spill. Misha didn't just love him, he idolized him. I can't find the words to convey how much Misha loved him. Ida said that if it wasn't for his father, Misha wouldn't have graduated from school, let alone university – he wouldn't have maintained the required diligence or patience, especially after he became obsessed with chess. By the way, it was Dr. Tal who introduced Misha to chess. He taught Misha the rules and at first beat him. This hurt the little boy's pride, and he immediately dived headlong into this mysterious game in which he kept losing to "Dad". I deliberately use the word "Dad" here, because Nekhemia Tal was the one and only father for Misha. And Misha's passport indicated Mikhail Tal's patronymic as "Nekhemyevich".

Meanwhile, during nearly all the years that I knew them, Robert also lived in the apartment. Tal also loved him and, as I have already noted, called him "Jack". Robert was Misha's biological father. Both Misha and Robert knew this. Nevertheless, as far as Misha was concerned Dr. Tal was his father, and as far as Robert was concerned Misha was Dr. Tal's son. This subject was taboo in the household. It was no business of friends or relatives and there was no need to demonstrate the truth to anybody.

I'm describing this unusual setup in the same words that Ida described it to me, so that the reader can appreciate just how atypical these people were. It was from this household that Mikhail Tal emerged, a man who did not fit any stereotypes.

Shortly after Yasha's birth, Dr. Tal was struck down by a powerful virus. This resulted in his complete and untreatable impotency – a tragedy that can often lead to the collapse of a family. However, the Tal family found an alternative solution, and those close to them never had an inkling of what had happened. Ida remained a young, busy woman, with an unquenchable thirst for life.

At that point, Robert appeared on the scene – he arrived from Paris like a charming Devil. Ida had known him when she lived in France. He was charismatic, intelligent and had great manners. Comme il faut, as they say. There shouldn't have been anything surprising about the fact that Ida fell in love with him. Perhaps a woman like Ida could have overcome a one-directional passion. Perhaps. But Robert soon fell head over heels for her. And the mutual gravitation of two people who have already experienced much in their lives is hard to resist. And should they resist, anyway?

So a love triangle appeared, and an apparently banal one at that. However, a banal love triangle requires secret dates, cheating, accusations, suspicions, scandals... Not in this case. All three participants were made out of a different fiber. Not like us! Nothing was announced but nothing was hidden... Robert appeared in the Tal household and Dr. Tal didn't require any explanation. It was a fact pertaining to the woman he loved and he accepted it with dignity, like a man.

Writing about the Tal family reminds me of Chernyshevsky's boring novel *What Is to Be Done?*, which we were forced to study in school. On the face of it, the situations were similar. Only without Vera Pavlovna's exalted speech and without the dull maxims of Chernyshevsky's male heroes...

Robert had divorced his wife, who lived in Germany with their young son (they were later murdered in a fascist concentration camp). He was fairly successful in business (in Soviet Latvia he was set to become a well-known trader), though this didn't prevent him from being jailed a few years after I met him.

Misha was born in 1936, the fruit of Robert and Ida's love. Everybody knew that Dr. Tal and his wife had given birth to a second son. And the rumors? So what? – Riga is full of rumors.

Ida told me that when she was seven months pregnant she was staying at the dacha by the Riga seashore. It was hot, the second half of summer. One night she lay down on a couch so low that she was almost touching the ground and covered herself with a thin sheet. Suddenly, a huge rat ran up to her face and she fainted in terror. The doctors were worried that the shock would impact her pregnancy.

Misha was born a frail child. He had two fingers missing from his right hand. When she first saw her son after he was brought to her and unwrapped from his swaddling clothes she again fainted in shock at the site of his three crooked fingers. She was unable to breastfeed. Her lack of milk was perhaps due to those shocks. She was treated for a long period of time after that.

When he was just six months old, Misha was struck by a nasty meningitis-like infection with a very high temperature and convulsions. The doctor said that his chances of making it were remote, but that survivors turn out to be remarkable people. Well, Misha began to read at the age of three, and by the age of five he was multiplying three-digit numbers – while adults were still struggling to solve the math with a pencil he would tell them the answer.

He got "infected" with chess at the age of seven and began to spend nearly all his time at the chess club, nagging adults to play him.

Robert was really the only person in the family who could have been described as wealthy. Misha, even after he became the celebrity Tal, never had vast amounts of cash. The clothes that he would bring back in abundance from foreign trips were always ordered by officials, especially those working in sports. Before each trip, they would give him lists of shopping. These would be "presents" – at Robert's expense, whereas the officials would not as a rule pay for anything.

Misha would splash the cash without counting it. He also loved treating people and giving real presents. He would never borrow money. People around him assumed he was rich – in fact, nobody doubted that for a second. Indeed, they were right!

Mikhail Tal! Nobody could have known that Mikhail Tal would spend every last coin, go to the post office and send a telegram to Riga: "Jack, please send another thousand." And the next day, Tal would again be rich.

It's also important to bear in mind that were it not for Robert, the entire Tal family could easily have perished in one of Hitler's concentration camps. Riga was always considered a "German" city, highly influenced by German culture and language. Everyone in the Tal family could speak German. And when the War began, Ida naively asked Robert: "Why do we have to leave? We're basically Germans. They won't touch us." To which Robert replied: "They won't touch Germans, but the will slaughter the Jews." And he convinced the family to evacuate to Siberia.

So they lived in this visible state of spiritual calm and equilibrium. Throw some stones into a stream and you will see the water lovingly wash every stone, big ones and small ones. None will be left out. In the Tal household, flowing between Dr. Tal and Robert, between Yasha and Misha, between Misha and me, caressing and smoothing out all the disagreements, Misha's mother was beyond doubt that stream. May she rest in peace!

Although I had by then been a frequent visitor to the home, it took time before I considered it to be *my* home. Each time that I came to visit, when I had dinner there and even when I spent the night there, I still felt like a fish out of water. I was constantly on edge. The conversation never turned to the question of marriage, even though we were apparently now engaged. That was fine for me – I had no desire to force events.

When Misha left for the 1959 candidates tournament in Yugoslavia (7 September - 29 October) I began to spend less time in his home. After shows or late rehearsals, I would return to my eight-square-meter room in the hostel. I continued to consider myself free of obligations and lived my own life. Just as I normally did. In Riga at the time, I had a lot of friends and acquaintances.

Most often, I went to visit Inna Mandelstam. She lived in an exquisite house frequented by well-known lawyers, doctors and poets. I only had to show up to be immediately sat at the piano and begged to play and sing for hours on end. Well, they didn't have to beg me for long – I loved to perform at Inna's home. There was nothing artificial about the intelligentsia spirit in the Mandelstam residence – it was natural and, probably, inherited. Inna's father was the first cousin of the poet Osip Mandelstam. Also, sometimes we would meet in a restaurant or take a trip to the seaside.

"Society" had by now doubled the attention that it paid to me. If an actor was drinking coffee with me in some cafe it meant only one thing – that I was having an "affair". People looked at me in the streets. Obviously, none of this was my fault. Actually, I enjoyed being noticed, eyed up and down. I even enjoyed people wanting to introduce themselves to me. I'm sorry, but show me a young and pretty woman who would be annoyed by that. If there is such a woman, to me it suggests that she has psychological or health problems. Well, I had no such problems.

Nor can I say that I was particularly agitated by the rumors. If anything, I found them amusing. Sometimes, I even acted up, knowing that I was being watched – I would demonstratively place my head on the shoulder of an old friend. The next day, everybody would be gossiping that I had a new affair. So you could say I was deliberately pouring petrol on the fire.

I really missed Misha. I was constantly informed how he was doing in Yugoslavia, whom he had defeated, how many points he had. However, as I mentioned earlier, I didn't understand any of that. People were saying that he had a real chance of becoming the candidate for the title of world champion.

Then, one morning, I received a letter for Yugoslavia. Mostly, Misha wasn't a fan of writing letters. He preferred phone calls. He simply didn't like writing. I have preserved only two of Misha's letters: the one from Yugoslavia and a second that I received from him in reply to my letter in which I asked for an official divorce. Curiously, many years later when my son and I left the Soviet Union, a story which I relate later, the customs officers pouring through our baggage found those letters and took great interest in reading them aloud. They then claimed that the letters could not be "exported" as they were "documents of historical importance"! Gera surreptitiously regained possession of those letters and hid them in his chest pocket. Once we had got through customs he proffered them to me and exclaimed: "Don't lose them! These are documents of historical importance!"

I include below an abridged version of Misha's letter from Zagreb. Sometimes, it feels like this peaceful time before we married never took place, like it's from a film from long ago, in which we didn't even play the main roles.

A good day to you, my darling!

At last, I have got some more news from you. It's awful – time goes so slowly that I can't imagine spending the remaining 18-19 days here. And the tournament participants are being asked to spend a week after it ends in Belgrade playing simuls. When Rogozin told me about this I informed him that it will be Sallynka's birthday (your name is already famous!) and that I have to be home. In truth, though, there's a small issue with the aircraft timetable. One airplane leaves on 31 October, but it seems that I won't catch it in time, as that's the day of the tournament's official closing. And after that the only plane with no changes, which goes Belgrade-Lvov-Moscow, leaves on the fourth. If I have to take that airplane you will need to be born one tiny day later.

But how about spending that evening in Moscow?! There are two options.

1. There's a route Belgrade-Budapest and then Budapest-Moscow on a TU-104. But that plane's timetable isn't yet clear.

And 2. I don't know but I may be able to bid farewell in Lvov to our entire group and fly from there (by the way, via Vilnius) straight home. Then I will arrive just in time.

My darling Sallunchik! How have you been in my absence?

...I never suspected that I would miss anybody so much, though thank God I have played decently at the tournament. You are my love, only my love, aren't you? Well it doesn't matter, baby, I'll arrive and then I'll be at home for ages and ages and will sit there and relax with you. Then on 30 November an international tournament begins in Riga called "The Baltic Sea – the Sea of Friendship", and, of course, Tal has to play there come what may, even though the sight of these wooden pieces provokes unpleasant impulses within me. But that's quite another matter – you will be beside me, and in that case playing chess will be a pleasure... And after that it's New Year. I think that by then we'll have recovered and we'll manage to celebrate it like before we were tied to each other! My dear, forgive me for not carrying out your request but in Zagreb material for an evening dress (taffeta) caught my eye so I took it. I think that you'll like it and you'll be my mermaid at New Year – the prince has fallen into the sea anyway! Oh, again I nearly forgot. I asked the people at home to send their orders, sizes (especially the latter) because I won't have any time for shopping. If they haven't asked you already then as soon as you get this letter write back to me or, to be quicker, phone me. Are you planning to speak to me? I'm already beginning to sulk.

It's time I finished. The last round in Zagreb begins in half an hour. Now that I've received a few scrawled lines from you, the result is quite clear to me. As you can see, I'm my usual modest self. I need to take this letter to the post office in time so that it flies off today to my darling, so that she gets it as quickly as possible and (who knows!), maybe she will even reply. I won't continue any more that I love you, love you passionately, I won't say that I'm missing you, that I want to be together with my red-headed little girl, I won't talk about being "chained to her with a tender passion"[9], I won't speak, I won't say anything! I will only say: see you soon, darling Sallynka! I'm waiting! (for everything). Send my best regards to your mum and dad, your friends in the theater, to our kind colleagues. I kiss you passionately. Always your Misha...

Misha had written this letter immediately after receiving my note that I had passed on to Zagreb via a diplomat whom we knew. My note was short, just saying that I was fine, that I forbade him to buy me anything (my girly pride!), that I missed him and wanted him to return as soon as possible. And that is why he apologized for not carrying out my request and "took" (a typical Commie-era expression) material for my dress. I should add that Misha hated shopping, yet he diligently fulfilled the many requests to bring all sorts of things. As I have already mentioned.

Several days after I received his letter, there was an early morning knock on the door of my hostel room. Barely aware of my surroundings (I'm not a morning person, like all artists), I opened the door to see Ida standing there. I had performed at

---

[9]   Words from a popular song at the time

a premiere the previous evening and had arrived home in the dead of night. The room was stuffed full of flowers, including the most luxurious lilies. It hadn't occurred to me to open the window and I was almost intoxicated by these lilies. I looked at Ida in alarm, thinking that something must have happened. I was quite sleepy as Ida hugged me tightly to her chest and said: "My daughter, get packing. I'm taking you to live with us. Forever..." A taxi driver showed up in an instant, carried out my case with all my "dowry" and loaded it into the car. And so that is how I moved "forever" into the home of my future husband, at 34 Gorky Street. I think that events had been speeded up in this way because both Misha and Ida had heard nasty rumors about me and, evidently, after Misha's latest phone call the family "council" had made a decision to take me under close control.

I was always struck by another of Tal's qualities. I repeat, *Tal's*, because he was Misha for me, for his family and for a small group of friends. For everybody else, he was a great and remarkable champion, a chess genius and an enigmatic character.

I am still surprised at the bluntness of many "mere mortals". They can simply walk up to a famous person in the street, in a hotel, wherever, and you're lucky if all they ask for is an autograph. They ask masses of questions, sometimes quite indiscreet ones. If the celebrity is a chess player they may question the correctness of a move from some game, or thrust papers into the celebrity's hands with the person's own opening analysis. Then other people claiming to have been a player's representative appear who explain in detail how, for example, they persuaded a stewardess to admit that player, a "blind drunk ex-world champion", onto her aircraft, convincing the gullible listeners just how caring they are. These people fail to realize that if a genius gets drunk, he gets drunk as a genius and remains a genius whether or not he has been drinking.

So what surprised me in Tal was the simplicity and naivety in his relations with such people. He could quietly engage in a chess discussion with a random passenger at the airport, and you even had to drag him away after the last call. He could be easily persuaded to play blitz in the park, and nobody could pull him away from that. Even if it began to rain he would simply ask the spectators to hold an umbrella over the board. Oh, and he could share a drink with somebody he didn't know if that guy seemed interesting.

I don't ever recall Tal saying anything tactless or rude that might have offended anybody. Were there people that Tal could have disliked? I don't think I met any. On the other hand, he liked to tease people. And the more Tal liked somebody, the more Tal teased him. He would constantly make fun of his friend and coach Alexander Koblencs. The Maestro (as everybody called him) never took offense. He acted as though Misha's jokes were addressed to somebody else and not to him. I heard a story that during analysis of a game a grandmaster made a sarcastic comment about Koblencs to his face. The Maestro looked up from the board and told his tormentor: "Tal never talks trash – he prefers to be witty. In your place, I would have come up with something witty."

Tal's jokes were always harmless. If he really did have angry words for somebody, that meant the end of their relationship, and the recipient would remember Tal's words for the rest of his life. In this case, though, the "offended party" would as a rule have deserved it. Also, Tal didn't like playing tricks on people. In his view, there was something humiliating about tricks. If somebody came out with a story about how a guy was tricked, Tal would raise his eyebrows and make a facial expression as though to say: "What was the point of that?"

Immediately after our official marriage, I tried to convince Misha to move into a separate apartment so that we could live independently of his family. I repeat: Ida, Robert and Yasha were all very nice to me, but nevertheless... Let me begin my saying that Yasha was a bit of a ladies' man, to put it mildly. Ida and Robert acted as though Yasha's private life wasn't their business. I, on the other hand, found this hard to take – I viewed Yasha through my female kaleidoscope as a hidden threat to my relations with Misha. The large living room was transformed into our bedroom, but Ida, Yasha or Robert would keep barging in, whether or not intentionally; Robert was sometimes overly concerned about Misha's health. And I was also quite tired of the young pioneers who kept showing up. Just imagine – almost every one of God's days that Misha was in Riga they would arrive at eight in the morning (the only time that Misha was available), and he would coach them while I made them tea and sandwiches. I would frequently tell myself: "Sally! I know you love children, but not *that* much!"

"Mishanka," I would say to him, "let's move somewhere else and live on our own. Our family. Just look at Averbakh, Botvinnik, Smyslov. They all have their own families, their own apartments. We'll buy nice furniture and hang cozy lights."

That was all in vain. It was impossible to persuade Misha to move. He could have obtained an apartment in Riga, he had offers to move to Moscow where he would be helped with finding a home. But no and no. Misha was used to living the way he did. He was happy with his setup and wanted us all to live together. It was comfortable from his point of view and shielded him from all possible problems. Misha didn't like problems – as an inwardly focused person they got in his way, and if they arose he genuinely believed that they should solve themselves. In any event, it wasn't down to him to solve them. Indeed, Robert and

Ida decided everything for him, especially Robert. If Misha left for Moscow, he would take money with him (a sizeable amount for those days), and after, say, a week, he would make the phone call I mentioned earlier: "Jack, please send another thousand!" Robert would say: "Misha, I'm happy to give you as much as you want, but you took a thousand roubles with you. Where are they?" "I don't know where they are," Misha would reply. "Please send me another thousand!" So Robert would send more money, and Misha really didn't have a clue how he managed to spend a thousand roubles.

Actually, if he went on trips without me, he would always be surrounded by an immense number of people – those who were his friends, those who weren't, and those who were chance passers-by. Female fans loved him in particular. Yeah, and Misha didn't exactly hate women either. Oh, and he would always act the gentleman: he insisted on paying for everything himself. He would fish out more money from his pockets and somebody would go and fetch some more brandy and cigarettes. Instead of one bottle, they would bring five (friends are generous with other people's money!). All the cash would go on drink, cigarettes and presents. And so the next call to Riga would soon follow: "Jack! I've run out of money."

No, Misha didn't want to live apart from his parents. Maybe he was even scared to.

Even before we got married I noticed that he would swallow handfuls of capsules. He would turn pale all of a sudden, screw up his face in pain, and then chuck a pile of capsules into his mouth. He would normally laugh off my questions as to what was hurting and what pills he was taking: "There is a guardian sitting inside me. If I ever lose myself in contemplation he shakes me by a straying nerve and tells me in my 'inner voice': 'You bad man! You have Saska!' And then I remember that there is nobody better in the world than Saska, and to thank him for reminding me of you I treat my guardian to his favorite capsules."

The doctor from the clinic where Misha was a patient told me: "He has something wrong with his lungs." Then it transpired that he had "something wrong" with his kidneys, too. But nobody could tell me what exactly. Meanwhile, sudden pains were grinding him down. During one attack he was diagnosed with "acute appendicitis", they placed him on the table, and... removed his perfectly healthy appendix.

However, I really came up against Misha's problems for the first time while he was preparing for the candidates tournament. He was coached by Koblencs and Averbakh, the latter arriving in Riga from Moscow. Even now, I fail to understand how he managed to prepare – he suffered from hellish pains just about every day. Misha was refusing to eat, and if we managed to convince him to eat anything at all it would have to be with a sizeable dose of brandy. Brandy to some extent reduced the pain. Some of his prep took place at the urological hospital to which we had sent Misha despite his desperate resistance. The specific smells and state of hygiene of that and all subsequent urological hospitals and departments leave me shuddering to this day.

Later, the well-known urologist Frumkin carried out a unique operation on his kidney. However, after two months passed the pains reappeared with venom and only injections of Pantopon could ease them.

...He has a wonderful ability with language and always has a sharp wit. I remember, for example, after a lecture some tactless dude asked Tal: "Is it true that you're a morphinist?" to which he instantly replied: "No, I'm a chigorinets!"

Yakov Damsky, *Riga Chess*, 1986

Some people believe even today that Tal was a drug addict. I still have a letter from Botvinnik in which, concerned at the health of such a leading player, he asks me to do everything within my powers "to cure Misha from morphine addiction." Botvinnik also believed that Tal was dependent on drugs. Well, I can state in all seriousness: Misha was no drug addict! He suffered abominable pains which nothing but morphine or Pantopon injections could relieve. Misha never went cold turkey demanding a needle —rather, he would double over in agony. There was no choice on such occasions. Yes, he took a massive amount of other pain killers. And he took all the measures he could to avoid drug dependence. He was afraid of becoming a junky and he avoided doing so. I'm sure that his predilection for brandy and almost non-stop smoking were for him an alternative to drugs as he struggled against the merciless, excruciating, destructive torture. His irregular pace of life and work also helped to take his mind off his physical suffering.

Petrosian once joked morbidly: "If I lived the way Tal does I would have died a long time ago. He's just like Iron Felix [10]."

Sometimes, it seems that Misha's life was an endless spin in some sort of Satanic orbit where effect becomes cause and cause becomes effect. And a beckoning star named Chess was at the very center of this orbit. Only death could stop this orbiting.

Generally speaking, when I project my mind back to those years, I sometimes ask myself: what would have happened had Misha not been a genius born to shake up the conservative chess world, one who burst onto its scene as a blinding comet to overthrow the chess sphinx Botvinnik and for many years after that to delight with his name not only chess fans but even

----

[10]   The nickname of Felix Dzerzhinsky, the founder of the KGB

those who had nothing to do with the game? What would have happened had Misha been an ordinary boy, witty, decently educated and well brought up? What would his family have made of their son's mad passion for me? Probably, endlessly loving their offspring (as is typical in a Jewish family!), they would have made every effort to prevent this "tacky little actress with a dubious reputation" from becoming the wife of their innocent and naive son, who from their point of view deserved a better pairing.

However, the issue was that Misha was a genius. Everyone who knew him was certain about that. Misha's phenomenal success in chess pointed to such a conclusion. So his parents, too, became totally convinced of this – and they began to implement the enormous mission that God himself had assigned them. They found themselves dependent on their son, whose every wish and fantasy became their unbending command. Therefore, if Misha loved Sally, they needed to draw Sally closer to them and they needed to shield Misha from any and all conversations that besmirched her reputation. I think that my moving into the Tal home was dictated by Misha, and that Ida and Robert carried out his demand to the letter. Still, being well brought up, they tried to convince me that they loved me no less than their son did. Another matter that, as time progressed, they accepted me and loved me as their own daughter. I felt their love even when our family broke up, first physically and then legally, and even after Misha started a new family. I also loved Robert and especially Ida throughout those years, and I continue to love them even today as though they are still alive.

After Ida moved me into their apartment I started to get calls from Belgrade just about every day, which I'm sure cost Misha a pretty penny. I feel too embarrassed to repeat all the lovey-dovey epithets he expressed in my address, all his declarations of love. I guess some people would have been damn envious...

We waited and waited for the plane from Belgrade. Not only had it not arrived but we were given no information about it. Lots of people had gathered at Riga airport to meet Tal. A huge party had been prepared to welcome him. Everybody knew that he had won first place in Yugoslavia and the right to play the world championship match. Eventually, there was an announcement that the airplane had been delayed for "technical reasons"[11], and Robert drove me home, as I had a morning show the next day and needed to get a good night's sleep. Naturally, I couldn't fall asleep. I suddenly realized that I was waiting for Misha's return like never before. And this made me really happy. I was sure that Misha would arrive as a different, renewed Misha, and that there wouldn't be any of those silly, unnecessary arguments that so exhausted us both each time. I expected his homecoming to open a magic door with a golden key to a peaceful future. I saw this future only in vague outlines, like in an early-morning fog that promised a warm, cloudless day. With tons of wonderful adventures that just thinking about took my breath away.

Misha eventually arrived early in the morning. The reason was muddled – either the aircraft had run out of fuel or its landing gear had failed to function. Misha, of course, made some witty remarks, said that the passengers were struck by panic, that a group of Orthodox Jews on the flight constantly prayed, and that he himself had a fit of nervous laughter, as he was sure that no accident would happen because any disaster would really sadden his Saska plus there would be nobody to

---

[11] Soviet-speak to mean that whatever the reason is the authorities feel no obligation to state it

defeat Botvinnik. I have already said that Misha liked to give everybody pet names. So, he called me "Saska". One day, he said to me: "Rembrandt had his Saskia, so I will have a little Saskia – Saska!" From then on, I became his Saska, and remained Saska to him throughout his life.

Misha unpacked his suitcases with their masses of presents and clothes bought to order for all sorts of people. The apartment turned into a mini-warehouse of branded garments. But the most interesting fact of all was that among the endless shirts, water-proof raincoats, outlandish (for that era) tights, shoes and medicines, there was almost nothing that he'd brought for himself, save a bunch of chess magazines.

Misha travelled abroad many times after that. He would bring back bursting suitcases, none of whose contents were his own. None of those goods would be sold on either, even though in those days selling goods brought from abroad made up a decent chunk of most travellers' income. It was all handed out, given as presents, delivered. Meanwhile, I would scour Riga's commission stores[12] to buy Misha shoes, shirts and suits.

Never in my life have I met a person who was so indifferent to their external appearance. He would forget to trim his nails (and a manicure was totally out of the question!), so I would have to catch him off-guard especially to carry out this important procedure. (By the way, the same procedure became an inherited "tragedy" for our son.) Sometimes, I would have to physically chase Misha into the bathroom so he would get washed. I would fill the bath with water, add bubble bath, and

---

[12] Stores that accepted new goods from private individuals on a sale or return basis for a commission, such goods sometimes being brought from abroad by those individuals

he would helplessly stand and behold the mound of froth and ask: "What should I wash first?" I think that the sole pleasure he got from bathing was when he sang opera arias in front of the mirror, of which he knew a huge number. Ida would repeat frequently: "My daughter! Can't you see how unworldly Misha is? He can go ten days without washing, yet doesn't he smell great!" Ida was of course exaggerating, but Misha really did have his unique, "unworldly" smell.

Basically, Misha returned from Yugoslavia excited, happy, as though flying through the air. Not long after, he said to me, as though in passing, "Sally, let's file documents with the registry office. It'll take six months or so for them to be approved. Is that sufficient time for you to be sure of your feelings?" He said this in a jokey way, stressing "to be sure of your feelings". I then asked him, switching to chess terminology, whether he had "miscalculated". He replied that it's only possible to miscalculate if you marry for money. And then he told me an anecdote: "Rabinovich, did you marry for love or money?" Rabinovich answers: "It must have been for love, because nobody gave me any money."

I got scared again. I was scared of losing my independence. I was scared that after becoming Tal's official wife I would be required to give up the theater, lose my freedom and become that same "typical chess wife". So I replied: "Why do we need to rush things? Why don't you play your match with Botvinnik and then we'll file our documents?" Misha laughed off my objection: "I get it. You want to marry the world champion, not the challenger!"

Ida approached me a bit later. "My daughter!" she said. "It's a match for the world championship! Why make Misha worry before his match? File the documents, and if you change your mind you can cancel your application after the match is over.

After all, we are all civilized people." So, I agreed. We held a big party to celebrate our engagement.

...I have seen several "births" of world champions: I witnessed the tragedy of Alekhine and the triumph of Euwe, Alekhine's return to the chess throne, the laurel wreaths placed on Botvinnik, Smyslov and again Botvinnik. But 7 May 1960 is one day I won't forget in a hurry. I have never seen such celebrations. It turns out that becoming world champion is physically dangerous.

At this happiest moment of his life, Tal wants to hug his mother and his young wife, but will those cruel photo correspondents and cameramen allow him through to his family?

"I want to go home," the exhausted Tal desires more than anything. It takes him a huge effort to break through the blockade of the throng of thousands and get into the car. Koblencs, Tal's second, is also happy. There are no more adjourned games, yet he has just as much to focus on as before: he has to protect Tal from the overexcited fans. All of this is happening in Moscow. One wonders, why are Muscovites so delighted? The Moscow chess world has been orphaned – the champion's residence has shifted to Riga. And if Tal is met by an ovation upon every step in Moscow, it's easy to guess what welcome awaits him in Riga. They say that Tal will return to Riga incognito, to avoid being torn apart by the crowds in happiness. Tal's multiple epithets, like "rocket" and "wizard", now have to co-exist with his venerable title "world champion". Mikhail Tal has broken all the records. You're not supposed to become world champion at 23. The great Lasker won it at 26, while other champions got there much later. Alekhine, for example, was 35. So Tal broke Lasker's record. Can he break Lasker's other record – his duration as world champion? We'll receive our first reply to that question in the return match with Botvinnik, if the ex-world champion exercises his right to challenge Tal.

...Misha Tal has been praised to the heavens in recent years. Now he could let it all go to his head. However, Tal is made from a different fiber. Even as the chess king he remains the same polite, witty, modest and charming man.

...Tal's happy mother says: "While Misha is the world champion he remains my child..."

Salo Flohr, *Ogoniok*, 1960

Misha made a phone call to Moscow and talked with somebody called Grisha. I heard him ask Grisha to come to Riga urgently to take some photos, as "Saska and I have decided to file documents with the registry office." Naturally, I enquired who this Grisha guy was and why we needed to be photographed filing our documents with the registry office. Misha replied that this was not some random guy but his friend Grigory Teitelbaum – a top photographer who worked in the magazine *Soviet Union.* I remember asking him: "Do you want the entire Soviet Union to hear about this 'historical moment'?" "Not the entire Soviet Union," Misha replied, "only its readers."

It was late December, and we prepared to head for the registry office. Misha had been grooming himself since the morning, which was totally unlike him: he put on a black suit, a white nylon shirt (the height of fashion in those days), and a tie. I thought this over the top, but I didn't react. By contrast, I put on a particularly modest grey skirt and a simple woolen blouse. Misha told me: "Saska, don't forget your internal passport. They might ask us for our internal passports." "OK, I thought, no harm in bringing my passport." Grisha Teitelbaum went with us. He had arrived from Moscow that morning and at the railway station in Riga he bought three luscious white chrysanthemums. Anyone who has visited Riga knows that beautiful flowers are always for sale there, at the railway station and at the famous indoor Riga market next to the station. Rigans always had a special place for flowers.

So the three of us showed up at the registry office. I was thinking: "If Grisha bought the flowers for me then why doesn't he present them to me?" We were met by a delightful elderly lady, and Misha said to her: "Tell me please, is the registry office director in his office?" "Yes," the lady replied, "in his office." "Please tell him," Misha continued, "that Mikhail Tal wants to speak with him." The lady disappeared and I asked Misha: "Since when have you had to file documents at the registry office with the director in person?" Misha replied: "Just to make sure, in case today isn't a day they normally accept documents. And once the director hears that Tal wants to speak with him, he won't say no." At that moment, the lady returned, acting ever so politely. "Comrade Director remembers that you phoned him and has been waiting for you since early morning." I looked at Misha and saw that he was a bit lost for words. "Saska," he said, "could we have phoned Comrade Director today?" "I didn't phone him," I answered. "Grisha! Did you phone him?" he asked, making some sign to Grisha with his eyes. "Oh yes, I just remembered!" Grisha replied. I called him... yesterday... from Moscow!" I felt something strange was happening, but I couldn't put my finger on it. Suddenly, Misha snatched my passport and darted into the director's office. Less than five minutes later, the director himself emerged, all smiles. Misha was hiding behind him. "My God, how beautiful!" the director exclaimed. "I congratulate you on becoming man and wife!"... I was speechless. Misha looked at me with smitten eyes and an expression on his face that a child has when he has given his darling Mummy what he thinks is an unexpected present. Meanwhile, the director continued to serve us: "Whose surname will you bear? Your maiden name or your husband's?" I nearly fainted upon hearing the word "husband".

I realized that all this was meant to happen, yet we had only gone there to file our application. I recalled Ida's words: *if you change your mind you have three months to withdraw your documents.* And suddenly "husband"! It seemed like an alien word, wooden. Grisha surreptitiously thrust the three white chrysanthemums into my hands and kissed me on the cheek. I couldn't find anything better to say than the quite out of place "joke": "White chrysanthemums are for burying in coffins." Yet the joyful director boomed "Exactly! From now on they will bury you from the point of view of other men and will let you live only for your husband!"

They then delicately enticed me into another room where a table stood covered with a fancy tablecloth and sporting fantastic long roses, champagne, fruit, and sweets. The director poured the champagne and made some speech about eternal happiness and bearing offspring. Everybody clinked glasses and I drank a glass out of shock and then a second straight away. Only after that I fully grasped the fact that it had happened: *Goodbye, Sally Landau! Welcome, Mrs. Tal...*

At this point, I thought: why do I have to bear Misha's surname? Why is mine any worse? Naively, I thought that by retaining my maiden name I would maintain my independence. I said to the director: "You were asking which surname I want to bear after marriage..." but here Misha interrupted me. "Of course, she will bear mine!" "We never doubted that for a moment!" declared the madly happy director, and he proffered me my passport, in which I could see the name "TAL" printed boldly.

I calmed down in the car on the way home: ultimately, everything's fine, everything's right and everything's wonderful.

I love Misha, Misha loves me. Only why did he have to speed up in such a theatrical way the start of our so-called "lawful marriage"? Misha seemed to read my mind. He kissed me and said: "Please understand, Saska, after today I have no doubt in my mind that I'll crush Botvinnik... and then..." (and then he sang from *The Internationale*) "...*The Earth shall rise on new foundations. We have been naught we shall be all...*" The most ridiculous thing of all was that our driver, an elderly Latvian (maybe one of the Latvian riflemen?) picked up in a booming voice: "*Tis the final conflict. Let each stand in his place...*"

Under the melody of the Party anthem we headed home. Ida opened the door and Misha said to her: "Murochka! Saska is now my wife!" That evening, we sat around the table in a small group: Misha and me, Ida, Robert, Yasha with his latest infatuation, and Grisha. Then various friends showed up. Even today, I consider that family dinner to have been our wedding party. Over the following days Riga accepted our marriage as a *fait accompli*.

As a rule, people accept even the most immense events and cataclysms more easily if they happen to somebody else. To be an observer is very different from being a participant. Naturally, all sorts of crazy rumors, gossip and made-up stories circulated. Some said I married Tal because I was six months pregnant and that he had no choice. There was another rumor that I was pregnant by somebody else. Yet another that Tal forced me to marry him, threatening to murder me if I didn't do as he said. God knows what else. Still, I don't know who cared about all that nonsense – I didn't. Ida, Robert and Yasha were tormented by both anonymous and non-anonymous phone calls, and at first there was tension and wariness in their attitude towards me. Misha's "uncle" was one of the few who didn't believe a word of those stories. By chance, I witnessed a conversation he had with Ida when he even spoke about me objectively and in complimentary terms.

I had found myself in the "epicenter of an earthquake". Marriage shook me to the core and I quickly morphed from a "young lass" into a "respectable wife" with an ensuing list of both pleasant and not so pleasant responsibilities. All my doubts fell away under the force of a mad passion that took hold of me. Society's rules no longer constrained either Misha or me.

We took delight in our new roles of husband and wife. I loved him madly and treated him as my very own, as part of me. A feeling of jealousy that I had never experienced before awoke within me and I started to react to all sorts of things that previously hadn't seemed to concern me. My inner Scorpio awoke – Misha should belong to me and only to me, not to Latvia, not to the Soviet Union, not to his parents and, of course, not to other women. Milunka Lazarevic, a talented chess player and, as I discovered later, a charming young lady, often phoned him from Yugoslavia. She and Misha would chat about chess. He would rattle off an endless number of variations in the secret language of chess notation, lining his dialogue with witticisms and exquisite compliments, at which he truly was a "grandmaster". After those calls I didn't sleep at night, tortured by suspicions. However, Misha was a Scorpio too, and everything had to serve or belong to him.

In time, I realized just how truthful the saying *diamond cut diamond* was. Or, as Marina Tsvetaeva wrote in one of her poems:

The strong with the strong are not fated to unite in this world...

This fact was to become the consistent reason for our arguments.

I had neither physical nor – even less so – emotional needs to cheat on him. And it was unthinkable to me that he would have such a need. But I knew one thing: if he were to be unfaithful I would do the same – twice. Simply out of frustration and humiliation. I certainly can't claim that such a trait of my character made it any easier to live, but I was born like that.

I worshiped and marveled at Misha. I would listen to him mesmerized. He would hold forth vividly, at ease, diving into new details while never letting go of the bigger picture. It was as though he were calculating variations while planning his next move at the board. Actually, this comparison occurred to me later. I often attended his lectures. He could speak for two hours, even three. While I would listen eagerly, and sometimes I felt that I even understood the advantages of the Scheveningen variation compared with the Dragon. I don't think he ever prepared for the lectures. Sometimes I would say to him: "Mishanka! Take a pencil, at least write down an outline – you've a three-hour lecture coming up!" And he would reply: "Saska! I chat with you for days on end, but I never need a pencil and don't write down any outline of our conversations! I'm not a writer, Saska, to put my thoughts down on paper, and I'm not an actor to then voice them aloud. I'm a *speaker*. Not a *loud* one but a *speaker*."

...On dozens of occasions, instead of looking up information in a fifty-year old chess publication, I would just call Riga, and Tal would instantly name over half-a-dozen moves played, for example, in the Soviet championship in 1939...
Yakov Damsky, *Riga Chess*, 1986

Tal was fantastically erudite when it came to literature, history and music. He liked to play the piano and did so marvelously, even while playing with his three fingers(!). He particularly liked playing Chopin, but didn't dare to play his favorite Rachmaninoff. Though he would flatter me: "Saska is our biggest expert on and lover of Rachmaninoff." After his first match with Botvinnik, a big concert was held in Misha's honor, and Bellochka Davidovich asked him: "Misha, what shall I play you?" He replied: "Rachmaninoff... but it should be at least as good as Saska's." I was really pleased that he said that, though I was clearly not as skilled on the piano as Bella Davidovich.

When the opportunity beckoned he would ask me to perform Rachmaninoff. Playing Elegie would put me in a particular mood. Rachmaninoff was also played at Misha's funeral, and it seemed like the ground was collapsing under my feet. This music has surrounded me my entire life, and today it seems like it was my and Misha's heavenly and wonderful destiny.

Misha possessed a phenomenal memory. Sometimes, we would compete: I also had an excellent memory, an acting professional's memory. I could read some poetry I didn't know, close the book and rattle it off without looking. Misha could also pick up new poetry, and if there were three poems on a page spread he would memorize all of them at once. He could read a whole book in one night, and sometimes two, although he obviously didn't know any special speed-reading methods.

There was artistry in everything he did. Although we never specifically discussed it, I think that deep down he would have liked to be a performer, winning the hearts of fans, the master of the entertainment hall. He adored audiences, he would transform completely when he saw that he was being watched and listened to, that his every word was lapped up. Sometimes, fully understanding that he was playing to the public, he would throw in some hidden meaning to the conversation, tactfully as

only he knew how. Not so much playing along as having people
on, enjoying the fact that he had hit the bullseye and provoked
a response.

Misha's pace of life was impossible for me to keep up with,
I didn't have the strength. If I tried to keep up I would drop
the ball on everything else: I would forget the simplest things,
I could put a skirt on inside out or leave my shoes in such a
place that I would never find them. Misha noticed nothing
of this, while tactful Robert would imperceptibly appear
alongside me and quietly say while looking out of the window,
as though not to me but to some empty space: "Sallynka, your
skirt is inside out. If that's the fashion then forget I mentioned
it..." I was quite upset with myself in such moments. I would
then end up with a monstrous migraine, which, by the way,
continues to torment me even today. I was astounded at
Misha's ferocious energy, not only when he was young, but
when he was fifty as well, when his body didn't have a living
organ left inside it.

Tal's unusual and powerful talent was best physically seen in
his eyes and his stare. This was particularly expressed when he
was deep in thought over the chess board.

Many people sensed – both tournament participants and
his fans – that when Tal projected his demonic stare onto the
chess board the pieces were energized by it. If an opponent's
piece was caught by his stare then it seemed like it was about
to catch fire.

The period of his preparation for his first match with
Botvinnik remains etched in my memory as some sort of endless
day full of tobacco rings, through which you could just make out
two silhouettes constantly moving the pieces up and down the
chess board and making notes in an exercise book from time to
time. I would go to bed, but Misha and Koblencs would continue

to move the wooden men. I would get up the next morning and they would still be sitting them, pushing the chessmen. Misha – unshaved, unwashed, uncombed, always with a Kent cigarette in his teeth – and Koblencs – well groomed, smartly dressed, looking quite the European (I still have no idea how he managed to put on fresh clothes and shave!).

I must confess, it's me who taught Misha to smoke. Previously, he couldn't stand the smell of tobacco, and would chase Robert out of the room if the latter lit up a cigarette in his presence (and Robert was a heavy smoker). While I began to smoke "out of necessity". I was playing the heroine in a modern play and had to smoke on stage. I had to rehearse smoking. Once, taking a full drag on stage, I felt my head spin, everything turned foggy and I almost fell into the orchestra's pit. However, I gradually got used to smoking, smoked a lot and even today I allow myself this "luxury", but only before bed. Misha didn't want to be outdone by me, so he also got hooked. Later, he would only need a lighter to light the first cigarette – all the others would be lit from the previous one.

I didn't get into the details of the upcoming match, as I knew I wouldn't understand anything anyway, but I heard conditions that Botvinnik was demanding being mentioned in some conversations. Misha treated those discussions as a joke, acting as the unquestionable future winner and hence accepting any terms. Once, he noted: "Even if Botvinnik comes up with the weirdest proposal I will accept. Firstly, because he's Botvinnik, and secondly, because I'll crush him anyway."

We all went – the entire family – to the match in Moscow, and were housed in the Hotel Moscow. During the match, I encountered a problem that until then I had considered non-existent: a nasty rhyme was thrust under our hotel door which stated that two Jews were playing for the glory of the Russian people. This really upset me, but Misha laughed it off: "What can we do? Only two people can play in the match." Generally, he didn't care about ethnic matters, though maybe he deliberately avoided them so as not to get upset.

In all probability, Tal really did see himself as a person without any particularly ethnicity, as a chess player belonging to the whole world. In any case, he considered the Soviet Union his homeland. Alik Bakh related how he had once spoken with Misha on the phone not long before his death – he was in hospital in Germany at the time – and Misha suddenly burst out with: "Please get me out of here, I want to die in my homeland."

Well, Misha won the match easily, never for a moment doubting that he would. At least that's how it seemed to me, though I understand nothing about chess. My father came to the closing ceremony from Vilnius. I remember saying to Ida as the laurel wreath was placed on Misha's neck: "That laurel really suits him, though it's a bit too big I think." My father overheard and noted, perhaps unfairly: "The wreath was evidently ordered with Botvinnik in mind and they didn't get round to measuring Tal."

Then a big concert was put on, where, as I said earlier, Bellochka Davidovich played Rachmaninoff...

I remember that throughout the match it wasn't the result that interested me so much as the number of brazen phone calls made to our hotel room. Mostly, it was good time girls calling. Moreover, they would say "Good day" or "Excuse me" but immediately "Please can I speak to Misha!" Misha would play along with them, making jokes, and I would die of jealousy. I shared this with Ida. She kissed me and said: "My little girl! He needs to have admirers. Firstly, because he's Tal, and secondly, see how handsome he is!"

Girls really did love Misha in those days, and they completely lost their mind once he opened his mouth and began to speak. But that was no consolation for me! I was crazy with jealousy and, unfortunately, as it soon turned out, not without reason. But I'll come to that later...

After the concert, we literally ran out of the Pushkin Theater where the match had taken place, via the back entrance. Otherwise, Misha would have been torn in pieces by his fans of both sexes. I don't know about the Soviet Union as a whole, but it seemed to me that in Moscow the vast majority wanted Misha to win.

We travelled to Riga by train. It's hard to describe in words what happened at the station when we arrived. Stills from the film showing the rejoicing Rigans carrying aloft the Volga with the happy but embarrassed Misha sitting inside circulated around the world.

Before going home, he went to the cemetery to the grave of Dr. Nekhemia Tal, whose patronymic he bore.

Almost immediately after the match, Misha began to suffer crippling pains and awful spasms, from which he had no relief either day or night. He would consume handfuls of pain-killers, but those and his injections only brought temporary respite. Both then and later, the doctors would shrug and say that he had "something wrong with his kidneys".

Some unusual things started to happen to me, too: I got nauseated, tired, other strange effects. Now I know that this was gestational toxicosis, but at that time I would spend days on end lying in bed, and Ida had no idea what to do with me. I thought I had a heart problem. Eventually, Robert insisted that I visit a gynecologist. He examined me and said: "Well, my dear, whom are you expecting? A boy or a girl?" "Nobody," I replied. "Then I've got news for you, my dear," he said. "You are about twelve weeks pregnant, congratulations."

By then, Misha was feeling a little better, and he and Ida went to the south of the country on holiday. They asked me to go with them, but firstly, I was busy at the theater, and, secondly, I felt pretty poorly. It's worth pointing out here that none of Misha, Ida or Robert had abandoned their idea of "releasing" me from the theater. But I stubbornly resisted: I was an actress and would continue to work there. Robert, leveraging his connections with the Latvian Communist Party Central Committee, even attempted to pressurize the theater management into firing me, but I was too good an actress to be fired easily.

Just before he left for the south, Misha suddenly claimed with a guilty-looking smile that the reason I didn't want to travel with them was that in their absence it would be easier for me to cheat on him(!). And he wasn't joking. I could see that and took offense, but I couldn't come up with anything more than to say that if I went with them to the south he would still find a way to "mingle with his admirers." I was jealous and so was he. But he was jealous in a different way: he, Ida, and Robert were genuinely convinced that I was solely Misha's property, while Misha belonged to everybody. I, however, believed that we had equal statuses: I belonged only to him and he belonged only to me. Well, the diamonds proved to be of equal strength – he and Ida left for the south, while I remained in Riga. Many years later, Ida was to admit to me: "My daughter! There wasn't a single day without all sorts of people calling me, some acquaintances and some whom I didn't know at all, just with the purpose of telling on you. Please forgive me, but sometimes I thought that they must have been telling the truth."

Aren't people evil! One actress who worked with my parents in the theater, whom I didn't know at all, who had left Lithuania for Poland in 1956, sent a letter to Ida from Poland once she learnt that I had married Misha (oh, and she didn't know Ida either), in which she "informed" her that "your darling daughter-in-law is just a neighborhood slut." And Misha read that letter, too.

His bachelor's instinct gained the upper hand − evidently, he decided that he had the right to "take revenge" on me. Unfortunately, in life you cannot take back a move and then re-continue the game. Well, maybe that's for the best. I told Misha and Ida that I was pregnant after they returned from vacation, although there was no particular need − it was obvious to the naked eye. Misha took this news without any particular emotion, as though I had bought him a new pair of shoes: "Saska, you are such a clever girl! I love you even more!" He hadn't matured enough to be a father.

Of course, I can't claim that I was a hundred percent ready for motherhood either, but I think that women discover their parental instinct earlier, and throughout life that instinct is more robust among mothers. I was already trying to imagine myself as a breast-feeding mother, I was worried about my unborn child − worried that he would catch some terrible illness, that they would have to operate on him in the hospital. I was worried that my son would inherit Misha's inexplicable pains (I was convinced from the beginning that I would give birth to a son). Basically, I was gradually morphing into a typical "Jewish mother". Add to that my sleepless nights driven by jealousy and you can see that my state of mind was far from calm and collected.

I began to notice that Misha was spending more time at the chess club than before. Moreover, at all sorts of hours, even when the club was meant to be closed. I couldn't let that pass. Misha stared at me with a meaningless smile, attempting to

find a more or less logical answer. However, he was a hopeless
liar – he kissed me and said naively: "You see, Saska, I have to
make a bunch of phone calls to various people and my voice
might annoy you. I cannot submit my Saska, who is bearing our
child, to such bestial torture." I made a face to pretend that his
answer was fully satisfactory. He believed me – I was a pretty
good actress, after all. Relieved and happy, he took off for the
chess club again, from where it was clear that his "bunch of
phone calls" would be made not to "various people", but just
to one...

I recalled how he had bombarded me with phone calls and
started to weep. And not for nothing. I don't want to name
Misha's passion at the time – firstly, it no longer matters today,
and, secondly, find me a woman who will needlessly name her
love rival. Even if it happened a very long time ago.

In reality, Misha had many female admirers, both before
me and while we were together, who included very talented
and intelligent women. Yet he always said: "My Saska plays
the piano better than Bellochka and dances better than Mira
Koltsova together with her entire *Beriozka* dance troupe."
However, he was attracted by quite different women. That same
N. was just a bad-mannered cow. Whenever we went to Moscow
she would shamelessly phone our hotel room and ask Misha to
meet him somewhere – and he would disappear to see her. Her
group of friends included hairdressers, black marketeers and
alcoholic performers of both sexes, and this gang would have a
good time spending Misha's money which Robert so diligently
sent whenever asked.

I recall Yasha saying: "It will end with Sally packing her
bags and leaving." Even Ida, for whom everything that Misha
did was right, started to worry that N. would drag Misha into
a quagmire. Whenever conversations of this ilk began in my

presence, Ida and Robert would switch to German, resembling plotters.

Well, this "plot" soon ceased to be a secret: with the help of Robert's connections, Ida complained to the relevant authorities, N. was placed under surveillance and she was eventually arrested and kicked out of Moscow. I only learnt this much later, from Ida herself, not long before her death. Then I thought: "If she had wanted, Ida could have got rid of me in the same way." For Misha's sake, Ida would stop at nothing when things turned critical. However, I was her son's favorite property and remained untouchable my whole life, all the more so as after Misha's affair with the actress L. (which I write about later) Ida really did start to treat me like a daughter.

Gera was born on 12 October 1960. He was about two weeks overdue, and Misha was awfully nervous. He was due to fly off for the Olympiad at Leipzig around this time. Several days before departure the team members gathered in Moscow and that was when I was admitted to hospital and gave birth. The other team members flew off to Leipzig, but Misha was allowed to return to Riga to take a look at his son (I was allowed to show him Gera through the window of the maternity hospital). Misha got really excited, cracked some jokes, but I don't think he had fully comprehended that he had become a father. Misha flew to Leipzig alone(!). It was hard to imagine this happening in those days. But it wasn't just chess fans who loved Misha. So did the authorities. At the very least, for a certain time.

Gera was a large new-born baby – weighing in at over 4 kilos, with a height of 56 centimeters. With completely ginger hair. A perfect copy of his mother. By the time Misha returned from Leipzig, we had already been allowed home. Misha took a look at this little ginger ball with a red bottom and was quite over the moon. It was as though he had never seen a baby before. Actually, that was probably quite true. He took great delight in examining his son in detail, continuously making new discoveries. "See here!" Misha exclaimed, "He has a real nose! And his lips! Look at his lips! And he recognized me straight away! See what a man he is!"

Yet despite all of Misha's joy, he didn't at first, in my opinion, perceive his son as a reality. More, he viewed him as an amusing toy. One after another, he came up with pet names: Bulochka[13] and Goose, Goosevich, Goosenysh. The name Bulochka got dropped as Gera grew, but Goose, Goosevich and Goosenysh remained throughout Misha's life.

I think that Misha properly realized that he had become a father the day that Gera took his first steps. He tried to maintain his balance for ages after I had placed him on the ground, then he attempted to move towards Misha, took some quick little steps and collapsed right on his father's knee, muttering "Papa" as he did so. Misha exclaimed that this boy was a phenomenon, a genius, that nature could create geniuses from ordinary parents, especially from ordinary mothers... Gera really did make a remarkable impression from his earliest childhood and was often capable of little tricks. He was less than three when I had to place him in kindergarten. He didn't like it, saying that there were "lots of cupboards there but none of them contained any books," and so he wouldn't go there anymore. I tried to explain that kindergarten was his work. Daddy worked as a chess player, Mummy worked in the theater, Murochka worked as a grandmother and Gerochka had to work in kindergarten. My exhortations made no impression on him whatsoever, and when

---

[13] Meaning a bun

I woke him up the next morning he exclaimed: "Kindergarten again?" "Yes, son," we agreed on this, to which he replied: "Then I'll protest by pooing myself again!" "Saska," Misha exclaimed, "we're bringing up a dissident!"

Did Misha love Goose? Oh, dearly. But did Misha give his Goose attention? Not much. Misha would have fun with him, but then Misha would seem to forget about him and go back to his chess. Then he would reappear, as though from another dimension, and then leave again. Goose was most upset by this.

Chapter 2

Gera (Goose, Goosevich, Goosenysh, Georgy Mikhailovich Tal, Father of Three Girls)

Twice a year — on my father's birthday in November and the anniversary of his death in June — I switch into a special mood. I try to postpone all important matters at work and come home early. A bottle of vodka awaits me in the fridge. I shut myself in the kitchen, place my father's portrait in front of me, light a candle, open the bottle, and my father and I start to drink, snack and chat from the heart, chat, chat... My children don't look in — my wife always finds something to occupy their minds. Praise her — she treats my rituals with proper understanding and sympathy.

In those years since he left us we have talked about all sorts of things. It seems to me that I've got to know him better than I knew him when we were in "physical" contact. However, I've also come to realize that I don't know him at all, no matter how bitter it is to acknowledge. Yes, I, the loving, honoring, idolizing son, don't know my own father. He doesn't fit into the usual framework of what we call a "father". Not at all. Yet it would be totally absurd to complain that he didn't spend much time with me or wasn't sufficiently interested in me. He was different. He loved me *in his own way*, passionately and sincerely. I was his son, but also *in his own way*. To demand that he love me like all fathers do, that he make a fuss over me like all fathers do, that he check my homework, that he lecture me how to behave — all that would be just as pointless as to demand that a natural-born

Englishman who knows no language other than his native one communicate with you exclusively in Russian, and not only in Russian, but in the Russian of Turgenev.

I'm a person of a totally materialistic world view. I buried my father, or, rather, I buried his body lying in a coffin, vested in an unfamiliar suit. I understood that my father *died*, that this was objective reality, yet I still have the feeling that he is playing in a chess tournament, somewhere far away from where it's difficult to send a message, but that someday he will emerge and I will hear his voice: "How are things, Goosenysh?... How am I? Bad, thank you. I'm on minus one, but if I win the last eight games then I will have plus seven, enough for second place, as Karpov will have plus eight!"

Now the pain has subsided a little, but at first I felt like my legs had been torn from me. I experienced phantom pains. My soul felt totally empty, with a large space previously occupied by my father. These circumstances – how to fill this emptiness in my soul – influenced my and my wife's decision to have another child. Another daughter was born, and we named her Michelle. At home we call her Misha. I look at her and I see my father in her, and I project onto her all the feelings I had for him. In medical terms, you can call this some sort of *compensation.*

My mother and father had their own particular relations, which I never attempted to grasp. When father married Gelya and Zhannochka was born, I treated that calmly, without emotion: Gelya was my father's wife, Zhannochka is my sister and Mum is my Mum. From the very start, I had a great relationship with Gelya and still do. Zhannochka remains my sole, darling sister.

Mum, like every mother, thinks that she knows everything about my relationship with my father. However, there was a period in my life, and in that of my father, which she knows little about. It was a period when all of Dad's ailments appeared at the same time.

It happened, I think, in 1989. It was a tough time in my life. I was on call in the clinic almost every day. We simply had no money. I even gave blood once a week, earning extra cash as a donor. So Gelya called me at work: my father had been urgently taken to hospital with significant internal bleeding, almost unconscious.

I call the hospital and talk with a wonderful doctor and wonderful man called Joseph Geikhman, who adored and worshipped Dad. He says: "The situation is critical. Although the bleeding has stopped for now it could restart at any time." I am the only doctor on call covering four wards. I cannot leave my hospital. Here is a challenge for a madman: either drop everything and dash to an apparently dying father, leaving my own hospital to the four winds, or remain in my hospital with the risk of being too late to see my father. I phone constantly.

They answer: no change at all, he nearly didn't make it to the morning. I call again. They answer: no change, he's still unconscious. I grab a taxi and head to their intensive care department. A man is lying there. He's meant to be my father, but he doesn't resemble him that much. The familiar face that I love, but at the same time it's not him. His face is quite grey. Some nervy people are running around him, and nobody can say anything coherent to me. Gelya is next to him, crying. Everybody is repeating one and the same: internal bleeding, they will hold a meeting to decide what to do. Then, Gelya and I are called into Geikhman's office and he says – his own eyes brimming with tears: "I don't want to upset you guys. Here's the X-ray. He's got a tumor." "A tumor? How can he have a tumor?" "Well there it is," he says, "an awful tumor in his stomach due to which you can hardly see his esophagus. That means we missed it earlier – there's no mistake in the picture."

They decide to operate urgently. Geikhman warns us that to carry out such an operation on a healthy person would be the equivalent of running him over with a tram car, let alone doing it on father after such a loss of blood. I offer to donate my own blood, but they look at my arms covered in pricks and say that they are not allowed to do that. I shout at them, threaten, demand that they pour my blood into him, pointing out that we have the same blood group and rhesus factor. They whisper among themselves, then place me on the table, extract my blood, pour it into Dad and take him away for the operation. My head is spinning after donating blood. They put me in a wheelchair and cart me off to the small balcony. "Sit there, breath some oxygen."

And sitting on this balcony, I pray for the first time in my life. No, not to God. To my father! "You have laughed at everything your entire life, you turned everything into a joke... I beseech you! Show us you are joking this time, too! Make everybody stupefied in amazement! You can do it!" I'm muttering but also thinking: how can he be joking with internal bleeding? Jokes when he's got a tumor?! I then head for the lift, and Gelya and I wait for the operation to end. Geikhman appears again. He has been standing next to my father throughout the operation, and he has the expression of a man who has just realized that he's a complete fool. "It's OK," he says, "it's not there. There's no tumor there... I don't know where it's gone... There's only a significantly eroded and inflamed stomach lining, and it bleeds whenever it's touched even lightly. We've blocked it with a medical sponge, given him more blood and are maintaining blood pressure."

Dad was wheeled off to intensive care, and, amazingly, after some time he started to exhibit signs of life, his face turned pink and he woke up.

"What are you hanging around here for, Goosenysh?" After a couple of days, he had made major progress. Some joke that was. Then I really said to myself: "Yeah, my Dad's from another planet."

Nevertheless, more "fun" awaited us. Father started to sit up in bed, read papers and magazines, and we did some crosswords together. He had no equal when it came to crosswords. However, at this point he was still so weak that after solving four or five words he would fall asleep again.

Two weeks later, I'm heading home from hospital duty and a friend is waiting for me at home with some brandy. He has returned from an expedition. We sit there working our way down the bottle. We haven't noticed that it's turned dark. Suddenly, the phone rings. I'm afraid of late calls, especially at night. Gelya is weeping into the receiver: "Dad's in hospital again." "What do you mean, 'again'?" "Didn't you know? He ran away from hospital?" "What do you mean, ran away?!" "He said he was bored. He put his raincoat on over his pajamas, surreptitiously ordered a taxi and went home. But our lift wasn't working. So he took the stairs up to our third-floor apartment. Before I knew it, he was happily drinking cabbage-flavored brine... Another basin-full of blood... They've just taken him away in the ambulance." I chuck what remains of the brandy into my bag just in case, grab a taxi and head to the hospital. Father is again totally pale and unconscious. This nasty thought races through my mind: "Why are you doing this, Dad? Why do you keep pulling at death's nose? Well, if you like those games then play them. But please take a break, we are only human."

And more of the same: blood, a transfusion, problems. Again, I had to argue with the anesthetists to persuade them to use my blood. And then I did something quite stupid and irresponsible. "What would my father really like right now?" I wondered. I ran into the toilet, drank the brandy and then lay down on the table. They extracted my blood and inserted it into my father almost straight away. Suddenly, I see his skin turn just slightly pink, like in the folk tale *The Scarlet Flower* [14]. After about five minutes, he opens his eyes, looks around and says, struggling to move his tongue, "Goose... I feel like I have just drunk brandy..."

So my father again got better, but with all the usual stiches and other "Tal joys". Doctors around him the whole time. The head   gastroenterologist of Latvia, a government minister, professor and really wonderful guy, was called in. He enters the intensive care unit, and my father, as usual, is smoking his Kent cigarette. The professor looks at him sternly and says: "Don't even think about giving up smoking." My father said later: "This guy can cure me. He understands me properly."

Well, my father had only just started to scrape through, and he was due to be transferred from intensive care to a normal ward, when Geikhman died. Suddenly, right at the hospital. A massive heart attack. He was lying in the very next room to father. Dad had this fantastic intuition. He got really nervous. "Please ask Joseph to come to see me." And how could we tell him that Joseph had just died? "He had to go home urgently," they told him. "He'll be back tomorrow." Tomorrow comes and there's still no Joseph. "He got ill," they tell father. "Pneumonia." Father is now on the verge of hysteria: "Tell me, what's with Joseph?" So we had to pump father with more

---

[14]   A Russian adaptation of Beauty and the Beast

Pantopon and tell him the truth. After that, he lay flat out
for a whole day, but then started improving steadily. As they
discharged him, he joked: "Thanks to your hospital I've totally
neglected chess."

But that was the last time he ever got better. Things went
downhill after that. They would stop for a while and then roll
further downhill.

The next time I saw my father was in Israel. We emigrated
on 30 January 1990, and two days later he made it to our place
in Netanya, together with Gelya and Zhannochka. It's like a
trick of my imagination. I remember it was a fantastic evening.
I took a lot of photos. Father was cracking jokes, drinking. We
were all laughing, acting silly. But something strange happened!
Several days later, I developed the photos, and looking at them I
saw a totally different person captured on them. Yes it was him,
Mikhail Tal, my father, whom just a week earlier I had hugged,
kissed, felt physically, but at the same time it wasn't him. It
was as though something vital, living, had left him. I thought
back to this parapsychologist I knew, who could tell whether a
person was dead or alive by looking at their photo. I showed the
photos to my wife, and she replied: "Listen, there's something
not right with your father." But I truly didn't believe, or didn't
want to believe, that something really terrible could happen to
him. I even told Nadia off and declared that my father would
live forever and nothing bad would ever happen to him. But I
knocked on wood at the same time.

Soon after, my father started to phone me. Well, actually he
had phoned me earlier, but only every month or two. Now, he
started to phone frequently, and I got worried about him. Our
relations were not what you would call orthodox. I had retained
a selfish attitude towards my father as my personal property
while I was little. I wanted us to live together, for my father to

spoil me and to take me to the theater and the zoo like "normal" fathers. However, I got used to the fact that this was impossible. And I was sad about that. However, after the age of 14 or 15, the feeling of sadness left me by itself. I realized that the frequency of "normal" relations between father and son didn't ultimately matter. There was a more important sensation: father was alive, father was healthy – he exists, he *is*...

Going back, this was one of our calls when I still lived in Latvia:

"Goosevich, hi! I'm in Riga. How are you?"

"Hi Daddy! For how long will you be here?"

"A couple of weeks. Why, have you had enough of me?"

"Oh, sure! I'll come over and see you tomorrow or the day after."

So I got to Gorky Street as fast as I could.

"Goose, I don't know if you've got smarter, but you've certainly grown. How are you?"

"Fine, and you?"

"Oh, great! I'm missing a kidney, screwed up at the tournament, lost money! Everything else is terrible."

Then he uttered a few more sentences and picked up a newspaper, while I watched TV and we sat next to each other. It was the feeling a dog has when his master is beside him. Even if he doesn't stroke the dog he is still next to him. He *is*. Not a twentieth century celebrity who happens to be my father, but simply my father. Actually, I was always embarrassed to have such a famous father and never used the privileges of a son of a famous parent. Whenever I was asked if I was the son of that very same Tal, I would reply that our surnames were a coincidence. I thought that if I said that my father was Mikhail Tal, I would be given undeserved benefits. I can't speak for other people, but I never felt comfortable receiving them.

However, I got anxious once he began these frequent calls. Moreover, his calls turned melancholic. He continued to make jokes (he couldn't hold a conversation without them), but his jokes now switched to hopelessness... Gallows humor...

"Dad, how do you feel?"

"Not too good... On the other hand, my abscess is doing great, much better than my tournament play in Spain."

"You need to come here to Israel to recover."

"Goose, I'm not an Arab to create another headache for Israel."

How Tal was Waved off to Israel

...Ex-world champion Mikhail Tal met up with a correspondent from Kommersant *and denied reports in the international press that he was emigrating. The rumor was started by major Yugoslav newspaper* Politika *which first reported that Tal was leaving the country, citing famous Soviet Grandmaster Alexei Suetin. That information made its way first to Holland and then across the ocean, where world champion Garry Kasparov happened to be at the time. Naturally, the champion was asked how serious Tal's intentions were. Kasparov replied that they were serious, and he provided a detailed version to the newspaper* New Russian Word: *Tal is extremely sick, his illness cannot be cured in the Soviet Union, hence he is leaving for Israel.*

The comments of such a famous and respected person are a sufficient basis for the information to travel widely. So the rumor about the Soviet Grandmaster's emigration reached newspapers in Sweden and the Federal Republic of Germany.

Tal commented Kasparov's declaration as follows:

"We all know Garry as a chess playing genius. Now we are getting to know him as a talented businessman and politician.

*But we couldn't have guessed just how erudite he is about Middle
Eastern medicine.*

*"I have a son in Israel, tons of friends, I travel there, I want to
and will travel there further. But always with a return ticket."*

Riga Chess, 1990

Gelya then called me: father's immune system had
deteriorated massively. "That's all we needed," I told her.
She continued that there had been some changes in his blood
composition, and did we have good hematologists. I replied
that we had lots of good doctors, including some very good
hematologists, and that she should send the test results by fax.

The results arrived. Our specialists read them and once again
couldn't understand a thing. At this point, Dad was suffering
from jaundice. Definitely not mechanical jaundice. And not
an obstruction. It seemed to be some sort of viral hepatitis. Yet
none of the samples revealed anything! A complete mystery!
He was as yellow as a lemon, yet his bilirubin level was normal!
Once again, all the laws of medicine flew out the window.

Once he calls me from Germany. I reply: "Father! You need
to get here as soon as possible."

"No way!" Then he changes the subject: "How's Nadia?
How's the weather?"

Gelya told me later that my father was afraid of going to
Israel – he had inculcated an inexplicable fear in himself. I think
he had no equals at convincing himself about things. Once in
Riga, he gathered us all at his apartment and declared as though
in passing: "For me, everything's finished. I will die in three or
four months. I have   cancer of the head of the pancreas.
So you can go on holiday to the south without me." And you
know what? Imagine that he began to lose weight, to reject food.
Basically, he decided to hurry up his journey to the otherworld

based on his self-diagnosis. Then he suddenly came out with: "It seems that I don't have cancer of the head of the pancreas after all." And he recovered! What "games" he would play.

I think that this fear of Israel was just another of his "games". I still feel guilty for being unable to destroy this "game", for not managing to persuade him to travel to Israel for treatment. Anyway, what's the point of all these hypothetical thoughts?... or of this "cultivating an old image", as my father liked to say? Tal wouldn't have been Tal if he didn't play his "game" all his life...

I went to Antwerp to visit my mother on 25 June 1992.

Mother has lived in Belgium for ages. After emigrating, she met a Belgian of mature years named Joe Kramarz. Joe was already a widower with two adult sons. He was said to have fallen in love with my mother at first glance, and I can well understand that. Even today, when I am 37 years old, she is an astoundingly alluring woman and it's impossible not to fall in love with her. And when Joe discovered that she was the ex-wife of that very same Tal, he declared that it was fate, that Tal was his all-time favorite chess player, that to meet Tal and perhaps play a game or two against him was his greatest wish... Basically, Joe soon asked for my mother's hand in marriage, and his greatest wish in life was granted: mother introduced him to Tal in 1981, and between then and Joe's death (he died of cancer nearly seven years after marrying my mother) they remained friends and even played the odd game.

So there I am at Mum's. I was quite worn out at the time and I simply wanted to rest and do nothing for a couple of weeks. It was the height of summer, beautiful weather, and mother said: "Let's go to the seaside, to Knokke. You can go swimming and sunbathe." Here was I, a resident of Israel, and she wanted to take me to the sea to sunbathe(!).

It's pointless arguing with my mother, and what's the problem, anyway? If she wants to go to Knokke then fine, Knokke it is. The very next day, we got into the car and drove to the seaside. However, neither the purpose of the trip nor the beautiful Belgian scenery put me in the right mood, as I kept replaying in my mind a nightmare I had experienced the night before: father swimming in a large pool. But instead of water, the pool was filled with blood.

Naturally, I said nothing of this to my mother. I tried to take my mind off it but I couldn't. Then, suddenly, mother says to me: "Gerochka, what are we going to do with your father?"

"What are you talking about?" I ask.

"I dreamt about your father last night and he was very sad. I feel really ill at ease."

It felt like being hit on the head with the back of an axe. I asked mother to stop the car. "Don't you feel well?" she asked. "You've turned quite pale!" I told her right there about my own nightmare. "We're both tired," mother told me. And we drove further. Until we reached the shore we didn't exchange another word.

We arrived, put our belongings away and went to sunbathe. We spent an hour lying there. But we couldn't enjoy ourselves, we weren't even getting a tan. We ate lunch. Mother says: "Let's go and take a nap. Maybe we haven't slept properly." It was about four p.m.. I couldn't fall asleep. I turned on the TV – normally I fall asleep quickly in front of the TV. No result. Suddenly, mother emerges from the bedroom. Looking all ready to leave, dressed, focused: "Gather your things, we're going home."

We arrive home, and Gelya calls us: father is in hospital and critically ill.

What were we supposed to do? We decided to phone the Russian embassy immediately. We found the numbers and began to call. Well, it was a Saturday. Somehow, we got through. We explained the situation. They asked us, do you have a Russian visa? No. Then we can't help at all. We tried calling again. We found some new numbers. At last, after about an hour and a half, we got through to a polite functionary. He was the consul's deputy or assistant or something. He said to come on Sunday, he would contact the consul. Basically, he promised to help. I remember him saying "we will help." Not "we will try to help," but "we will help."

However, a bureaucratic procedure awaited me at the embassy: approvals and so on. "We can't help you at all." I was close to tears: "Look, this is an exception. My father is going to die, please do us a favor." I asked what exactly was needed to be granted a visa. The reply: "An official telex from the chess federation confirming what you told us, and a letter from the hospital." I called Gelya in Moscow, and fifteen minutes later the embassy fax machine printed a letter from the hospital. "Where's the round seal? Where's the telex?" More tension, more approvals.

At last, I was granted a visa: "But bear in mind it's an urgent visa, it costs twice as much." So what? Let it cost four times as much!

I was on the next flight to Moscow.

Throughout the flight, I endlessly smoked and prayed. I prayed to both God and my father. Essentially, I was praying that my father would "laugh it off" this time, too. However, my dark presentiments were stronger than my prayers, and the closer we got to Moscow, the more distinctly I felt that this time there was no more joking to be had. Previously whenever he had ended up in intensive care, I had drawn bright pictures of the future: I imagined him getting better, and once he was fine he would again set off for tournaments. This time, however, like a compilation film with no chronological sequence, random episodes from the past, bits of conversations and odd details linked to my father ran through my mind, serving to convince me further that there was no way back.

Vague memories from my childhood again appeared out of nowhere. I was comfy on my little bed in our apartment in Riga, with Dad sitting on the edge and reading me a book. I can't remember which one. Yet I hear his voice succinctly. Why I had been visited by this unusual episode right then I don't know. My father didn't have much time to spare, and he read to me quite rarely, though today I can say with absolute certainty: I gained huge pleasure when he read to me, but he gained even more.

I tried in vain to recall any occasion when Dad might have punished me or even shouted at me, though I cannot say that he spoilt me. He would never give me moral lessons or lecture me how to live. He once told me off, it's true, but in his own way. He took me with him to the Keres Memorial in Tallinn. There were a lot of masters and even grandmasters on the train, and after people woke up in the morning, as is normally the case, they gathered in the train corridor while chatting and awaiting their turn for the toilet or smoking.

I was fourteen, but had taken up smoking at thirteen. I told my father straight away. He immediately proffered me a cigarette and stated: "I don't believe you. Go on, take a drag." And when I drew on the cigarette he said to me seriously: "Now I believe you." Then he brought out an entire block of Philip Morris cigarettes from the table drawer (this was a present fit for a king in those days!) and concluded solemnly: "It's better to smoke very good quality cigarettes openly than some rubbish hiding in the stairwell."

So I approached my father in that train, and, like an equal, asked him for a smoke. Tal's son, just a young lad, brazenly asking his father for a cigarette! My father put on an exaggeratedly strict face and asked: "Have you cleaned your teeth?" "Not yet," I answered. "Who brought you up?" he pronounced in a teacher's tone. "First, brush your teeth, and only then smoke a cigarette – with *clean* teeth!"

My flashbacks included my father returning home from tournaments with presents. He would never return without a present, and in fact I treated his every homecoming as a present. The presents could be chaotic, unsystematic. Sometimes, I was too old for them, at other times too young, in which case I would express confusion. My father would say, "for when you're older."

As I mentioned earlier, sometimes I was upset that my Dad was different to all the others, that he didn't take me to the zoo, cinema or theater on weekends. By the time I was ten, mother and I lived separately from father. He would leave for his tournaments, and I again celebrated my birthday without him, and without his presents. And then while he was away we stopped hearing from him. So one day after he returned from that tournament I called his apartment and told Robert that I was quite offended, that I wouldn't ever come and see my father again, and so on. I got quite wound up and hung up. My father called back an hour later: "Goosevich? Forgive me, darling! Your Dad got exhausted from playing... But I was thinking about you all the time... You know how hard it is to call you from abroad... Forgive me, Goosevich, or should I go and drown myself?" And then I felt shame at having taking offense at him. I went straight to Gorky Street and apologized. Dad acted as though nothing had happened, and ever since then I lost my "selfishness" as a son. It was then that I realized in an adult sort of way that this was the father I had, and no other!

A lump appears in my throat when I realize that I will no longer hear "Goose", "Goosevich", and "Goosenysh" that I'm so used to. I always thought that if my father died, "Goose", "Goosevich", and "Goosenysh" would also disappear. And that a new, quite harsh period of my life would begin. Had I lived alone, I would probably have burst into tears. But then I thought, did my father ever call me by my name? Not Goose, but Gera? I couldn't recall a single case. Once, he addressed me as Gerusha... I remember it well, it was in autumn 1980 in Amsterdam, when we visited him before he played at the Interpolis tournament in Tilburg, bringing some presents for my Nadia, who had remained in Riga for the time being.

Life was tough for me at that time. My mother and I had by then been living – or more accurately existing – in Germany for over a year. I hadn't found any proper work and I couldn't arrange any studies. I love Nadia, she's supposed to be my fiancee. I'm in Germany. She's in Riga. What will happen next is unclear. I'm feeling torn apart. Basically, I have lots of good reasons to feel nostalgic. And Mum said to me: "If you are suffering so much, why don't you go back? You'll sort things out with Nadia and then you can decide what to do next..."

Well, it was easy to say "why don't you go back?" in those years!

So we came to visit my father in Amsterdam with presents and I had some very serious questions. That evening in his hotel room, I told him that I planned to return and, naturally, that I needed his help in this. Well, that was the first and only time in my life that he called me Gerusha. "Gerusha, I realize that you want a ready reply from me and a solution to a task posed to you by *another* person, even if that *other* person is your father... But no. You need to create the task *yourself*, and then I will try and help you to solve it technically no matter what the task is." I replied: "I'm coming back." Father stared at me with penetrating eyes. (It was the same look that he projected at opponents during games.) Then he said: "Don't rush. Don't make a move that you risk having to retract. First, I'll help you with a visitor's visa, and then we'll see. If you then want to remain, you will." Basically, he wanted to say that if I then wanted to remain he would help me to do so.

Whenever I weighed him down with my problems he would try to go through them calmly, focusing on the real circumstances. (In his relations with me, he realistically assessed the difficulties, as though they had been caused by an opponent over the board.) That happened for the first time at the end of 1978. Nadia and I had returned from Sochi after a holiday, and Mum had told me of her plan to leave the USSR, which was a total surprise for me. At the time, I had neither a desire nor a reason to leave: I hadn't completed my degree, while a passionate romance was blossoming. I was shocked and told her: "File your documents, but I'm staying... At least until I graduate and marry."

However, when she applied to leave, the Soviet authorities told her bluntly: "Don't think for one second, citizen Landau, that we are total idiots. First you will leave, and then your son will follow. But we have no intention of training specialists or soldiers for your Israel. So kindly leave together or not at all."

So then I decided to apply to leave as well, as I was duty bound to help mother. She meant too much in my life, and I was ready to sacrifice everything for her. I hoped that I could later return and meet all my obligations to Nadia, without whom I couldn't imagine my life at the time.

Yet without my father's formal approval, that he didn't object to his son leaving permanently for the state of Israel, I would not have been allowed to leave. This was because mother was going to leave on an Israeli visa, which meant we would be emigrating.[15]

As soon as my father learnt of mother's decision he said without a moment's thought: "If Goose doesn't object then nor do I." He was perfectly aware of the difficulties that our leaving could cause him. Fast forwarding, Nadia's brother, who worked in Moscow in a scientific research institution, was fired from his job soon after we left. That's despite that fact that at that point Nadia and I still had no formal ties. Whereas I was Tal's son! Of course, on the one hand, my father was no ordinary father, but an international star. On the other hand, his glory years were behind him. The country had created new, more compliant idols, and the government and party's love for one of its ex-world champions had waned. Despite all his unworldliness, father clearly knew what he was asking for, yet he could not have acted any other way. "Do you really think that during the game we won't manage to work through the difficulties as they arise?" he would often repeat.

Dad was one of those people who take decisions quickly and solely as their conscience advises them. He would deal with the consequences later... After I flew back to Riga on a guest's visa in November 1980 for two weeks, where I soon decided to return there permanently, Robert told me: "I'm glad that you are returning, but you need to realize that you are coming back to a cage." And this was said by the same man who had considerably helped me to escape from this cage, both financially and through moral support, just a year and a half earlier. Father reacted calmly: "If that's your decision, then stay. I will do everything

---

[15] Permission was required from both parents under such a procedure even if the person emigrating was an adult

I promised." And he did it. That said, Gelya took upon herself the hassle with restoring my place in the institute, registration and finding me an apartment, and I will be eternally grateful to her for that.

Back to 1992. The closer the aircraft approached Moscow, the more anxious I became. I couldn't imagine life without him. And I felt more than ever before how madly I loved my father. My love for him only became clear when I was already an adult... Did I love him in my childhood? Maybe, just as children love their fathers, but at the same time I didn't love him, because, as I now realize, his relationship with my mother, and, by inference, with me, could hardly be described as normal. I remember mother and I living together in a room in the apartment on Gorky Street while Dad lived with some lady in another room. I guessed that this wasn't what people were supposed to do, but accepted it as reality, because I knew that I could go and see Dad in his room at any moment and he would always be glad to see me.

I remember clearly leaving the apartment with mother one ordinary day. We took the stairs, as the lift was broken, and mother suddenly said: "My darling, your Dad and I have to divorce. You need to decide with whom you will live – with me or with Dad." What did I understand at the time? Nothing. And today I can say that the question that mother asked me wasn't a fair one. Nothing depended on me. I lived with mother and believed that I should live with mother, and I realized that after the "divorce" I would see my father just as often as before this "divorce". I had no concept of a "normal" family.

At one point before this "divorce", when mother went on a long tour while father left to play some tournaments, I suddenly found myself sent to stay at a camp on the seaside. But it seemed to be a children's home too, with all the children sporting shaved heads and wearing homogenous grey frocks and suits. To this day I don't know why I was "exiled" to that place. I hated it and cried frequently. Dad came to visit once, for the whole day. He brought me a wind-up toy ambulance (and this has stuck in my mind my entire life) with flashing lights and a siren. I remember he took me to a restaurant and the circus. I remember having a fit when he left. I was hugely distressed that other children lived with their mums and dads *all the time*, while I always had my mum or dad going travelling, and sometimes the two of them at the same time. So I was quite prepared for the "divorce" in that sense.

At the age of about ten, I was hospitalized with some illness. When my father came to visit, the doctor asked him to play chess with me so that all the ill children could watch. By that time I had learnt a bit about chess – at least, I could move the pieces. I remember my father agreeing and "losing" to me as the believing audience watched. The naive doctor was so shocked by the result that he tried to persuade Dad to bring me up as a chess player. My father, smiling, replied: "Two madmen in the same family is too much!"

Fragments of an interview given by Mikhail Tal to correspondent of the weekly Nedelya *Georgy Kofman (1973)*

G.K.: We have listed your official titles, but obviously there are others, too. For example, Yugoslav chess correspondent Nedelkovic wrote that foreign fans call you the Chess Wizard, Rigan Pirate, or the Demon of 64 Squares. So I don't even know how to address you!

Tal: Just call me Misha! Firstly, because that's how I'm normally addressed, and, secondly, so that I don't feel I'm getting older!

G.K.: Let's try to "play" in your style: a frontal attack. Headings appear in foreign publications such as: The Re-birth of Tal, A New Spring for the Rigan, and Can We Expect a Tal-Fischer Match?

Many chess journalists, given that according to Professor Elo's coefficient you are ranked second after Fischer, are hoping for that. What about you?

Tal: I'm also a journalist, and obviously I'm in solidarity with them. But their and my passionate desire isn't enough to make it happen!

G.K.: Nevertheless... Remind me of your score against Fischer.

Tal: Well, those games are only of bibliographic importance. We played in the days when it was my name that scared little children, not Fischer's. The last time was in 1962. Of eleven games I won four, Bobby won two and the other five were drawn. Since then, Fischer, who is beyond doubt both talented and hard-working, has become one of the greatest figures in the modern chess world.

G.K.: What was the most unusual chess game you played?

Tal: Fairly recently, against Paul Morphy. Yes, I'm not joking. A well-known psychiatrist invited me over and asked me to play... Paul Morphy (do you remember the name of the first American champion?). The doctor had hypnotized some lad and convinced him that he was Morphy. He was so hypnotized that he agreed to play me only for 100,000 dollars. The "fee" was handed to him by the doctor (a blank piece of paper, of course), and we sat down to play. "Morphy" played much better than later, when he once again turned into a Moscow lad and had forgotten what had happened to him just half an hour earlier. Still, as "Morphy" he lost three games to me.

G.K.: Has your son Gera followed his father's example? Does he play?

Tal: No. He tells me that he has more serious things to do.

G.K.: What do you think of chess in the USA?

Tal: A comment by my favorite Ilf and Petrov inadvertently comes to mind: "One-story America" — skyscrapers over there

like Fischer (the highest of them all!) – one, two, three, four, and
you've run out... The chess boom that began there after Reykjavik
is subsiding, while the Soviet Union remains a country where the art
of chess, I would even say the music of chess, is loved, valued and
understood by millions of people. Our resources are inexhaustible!

G.K: So you're an optimist?

Tal: Based on a sober calculation of a decent set of possible
variations!

To be fair, I will say that mother nature bypassed me
completely when it came to chess talent, so it's a good thing
that I was never infected by the illness of chess – Tal Junior
would have been a total embarrassment to Tal Senior. Actually,
when I was about 18 I got into suicide chess and achieved
quite impressive results. Then I learnt that this was a totally
"legitimate" game: it had its own theory, text books and even
championships. I once challenged my father to a game. He told
me that suicide chess was good for holding a tournament among
psychiatric hospitals, but he agreed to play. I crushed him, he
muttered, "what a load of nonsense," thought for a little and
suggested playing again. He won. After that, we played a number
of times and I can proudly say that each time we played five
games the result would be 3:2, either in my favor or his. Except
that if he consumed a glass of vodka he would leave me with no
chances.

He would get drunk quickly. With his health, he didn't need
much, but the strange thing was that after he had reached an
initial high he could drink a lot without getting "worse". He
might get drowsy or fall asleep at the table if he was also tired.

And not one person who encountered a drunk Tal can
say that he became unpleasant, nasty, aggressive or lost his
judgement. He never caused trouble for anybody. People

adored him in whatever state he was and treated him like he was sacred. Even those people who saw him in that state for the first time.

I was so preoccupied with these and other thoughts about my father that the flight seemed really quick. Upon arrival, the passport and customs formalities didn't seem to be any burden either. Maybe in my absence from Russia there really had been some changes for the better. I don't remember what I thought of Moscow. "Photographic" clarity of vision appeared in the hospital, though.

Though what clarity of vision? The following days were like driving through fog. Fog, fog and more fog, and then suddenly some light, the sun, the contours of a landscape, absolute clarity, and then once again nothing but fog.

I look through the window of the information desk. A lad and two lasses are sitting in white overalls, discussing something. I apologize and wish them good day. They look at me with some annoyance − I had interrupted their chat. However, something in my eyes must have appeared sufficiently serious, and one of the lasses asked me coldly but politely, what I was looking for.

"I want to see my father."

"Where is he?"

"In intensive care."

"They won't let you in."

"They will, which way is it?"

"Your father's surname?"

"Tal."

"Let me check" (dials a number). "Where is Tal?"

"Oh?"... (a pause). "OK, I'll try"... (she turns to me). "I... have... to tell you..."

"When?!"

"Three hours ago... You can go up there..."

A fog... The anesthetist: "I can't let you in... We haven't tidied up yet..."

"How did it happen?"

"Profuse bleeding...... Esophageal varices..."

"Thank you... Forgive me..."

I apologized because I had started crying... I turned to go and he said to me: "He was waiting for you... And when he was conscious he was asking for you."

These words still ring in my ears today and will ring in them until my final hour.

And then, we were at Semyon's apartment, father's friend. Father had been particularly close to him at the end. Semyon, his wife, Zhenya Bebchuk, Gelya, Zhanna. Only Zhanna was crying. Thin, worn out. Nobody else was crying, I remember clearly. And for some reason everybody was trying to recall funny stories from father's life. As though he hadn't died, but had just left for the next room and was about to return.

So that's the person that he was: almost nobody cried even the day he died. Our shock was expressed paradoxically – we were all recalling something funny.

After that, complete chaos ensued. I thought: "How fortunate that mother didn't come. Despite her resilience that's the last thing we would have needed."

Again, fog. And then a conversation in the morgue with the attendant: "Don't worry, we'll do everything perfectly. We know who Mikhail Tal is!"

A total fog as we brought his body to Latvia. And here, I am particularly grateful to Anatoly Karpov. If it wasn't for his influence and insistence, I don't know how we would have managed. He organized everything – the transportation and even an escort of motorbikes.

Then more fog during the journey from the station on the bus, which stalled every two hundred meters. As it started to drive up Riga's famous Gaisa Bridge the bus predictably stalled again, and I remember having only one thought — how to hold the coffin so that father didn't get car sick(!). I refused to believe that he was dead. I still don't believe it. At the time, it seemed like a nightmare with a farcical comedy, during which father was travelling to Riga while lying in a coffin.

My father was a national hero in Latvia. And I expected huge crowds at his funeral. It was a rainy and gloomy day. I guess several hundred people showed up at the cemetery. Of course, that's a lot, but certainly not "huge crowds". Obviously, I was unconcerned about the number of attendees — I was there to bid farewell to my father. But I subconsciously felt some disappointment — after all, I had expected "all of Riga" to come and pay their respects to Tal, and when he returned with his champions laurels "all of Riga" did meet him. I had read the newspaper reports, Mum and other witnesses told me about it. On the day of the funeral I felt my father had been a bit let down.

I recalled a scene from my childhood. Looking out the window I saw a large flock of pigeons land on the ground. They were running around one pigeon that was having a seizure, and I had the impression that they were genuinely concerned about their comrade's wellbeing. But... they held a "discussion" among themselves and those at the back pushed their way closer to watch their companion die. The dying bird convulsed a couple of times and stopped moving. The wind blew and some feathers fluttered from the dead bird. The pigeons purposefully flew off in various directions — their dead comrade was no longer of interest to them. Well, that often happens with people, too, but I didn't want that to happen to my father. Unfortunately, I think it did.

For me, for Mum, for Gelya, for Zhanna, maybe for another dozen or so people who were close, this gaping emptiness that appeared when my father departed this world will remain until the end of our lives, one which nobody and nothing will fill.

At the funeral, I remember Alexander Bakh crying like a child. I remember Ratko Knezevic, whose face expressed total disbelief at what had happened. As he later himself said, he couldn't grasp its meaning, just repeating to himself all the time: Misha died, Misha died. But the awareness that his friend Misha had died, that the great Tal had died, didn't get through to him. It seemed impossible to him, because it would never be possible.

I also remember Alexander Koblencs, who was simultaneously saying lots of kind things about my father but at the same time saying all sorts of absurd things quite incongruous with the fact that my father was lying there in a coffin.

For some reason, I even remember an idiotic functionary declaiming official mourning nonsense. I really wanted him to shut up. Then, a strange discussion began on whether or not to place a chess set in the coffin. I think they decided against the idea. Who cares? Now it certainly is of no consequence.

Then another reality dawned on me: our big family had suddenly disintegrated.

I live and work in Israel. On my way to work I pass a cemetery every day and am reminded that the cemetery where my father is buried is far away and I can't just go and visit his grave. Each time, I reproach myself for not forcing him to come to Israel, where, perhaps, we could have extended his life, or, if not, he would at least have been near me. This isn't selfishness. It's my pain. It's my link to my father.

For a year after father left (I still cannot say "my father's death"), whenever I found myself in a restaurant or cafe I would consistently order a shot of whisky or brandy, then a second, then a third, and I would launch into a long conversation with my father, physically sensing his presence. Earlier, he often called me in my dreams. It happens less often now. I sit next to him. Sometimes, he hugs me, or strokes or kisses me, and I feel him physically, with the palpable contact with him that I so badly needed when he was alive.

Many people spoke and wrote about Dad's illnesses. Tal could not be thought of separately from his "pains". Yet nobody could say anything sensible. When I was about 23, Ratko Knezevic found a ridiculous article in a Yugoslav newspaper stating that Mikhail Tal had spent a long time in hospital with irreparable cirrhosis of the liver and atrophy of the kidneys, but that he had lately been put back on his feet after he had received a kidney transplant from his brother Yasha. We were all left dumbfounded by the article: by the time it appeared Yasha had been dead for three years, and Dad acted like he was furious – why had nobody told him that he had received Yasha's kidney? He "would demand that Yasha be exhumed"... I guess this was really his black humor. But Dad really loved his brother, and Yasha, to whose resting we raised a toast, surely "forgave" him in the otherworld.

Well, the actual start of all my father's physical ailments, however banal it may sound, was the fact of his birth. Ever since then he simply collected illnesses. But the fundamental cause of course was his totally pathological, nephrotic kidney. It tortured him relentlessly. People suffering from kidney disease know that there is nothing worse in the world than pains in the kidneys. I don't understand how such people can even exist, let alone play chess. I'm sure that it wasn't my father who lost the return match to Botvinnik, but his diseased kidney.

Yes, he was given pain-killing injections. There is no doubt that this caused habituation. By the way, it also provoked various claims and rumors that Mikhail Tal was a hypochondriac, that actually he didn't have anything wrong with him, apart from being an alcoholic and a drug addict. When this "alcoholic and drug addict" was placed on the operating table in Tbilisi, the doctors were amazed that this "hypochondriac" was still alive! What they found during the operation could scarcely be termed a kidney – it was like some melted necrotic mishmash all the way through. Father remained with one kidney, which eventually compensated for the missing one, hypertrophied and so on.

The doctors forbade him from smoking and drinking... from living. How could he survive without that!

My father treated his life like a chess game, somewhat philosophically. There's the opening, then the opening transposes into the middle game, and if no disaster strikes in the middle game you get into a dull, technical endgame, in which ultimately a person has zero chances. As far as I know, father didn't gain pleasure from playing endgames – he found them boring and insipid. Force him to give up smoking, brandy, partying and female admirers – basically, the source of intense experiences in the middle game of life – and he would find himself in the endgame, when he would have nothing left to do other than passively see out the rest of his life. However, that would have been a different person just resembling Tal. And what's the difference – to die spiritually or die physically if you can no longer be Tal? He had beyond doubt calculated this long combination with a large number of lines. He realized that he couldn't outplay death, but that he could still make mischief big time and would yank death boldly by the nose.

"Making mischief" was his favorite expression. I observed him once when he and Koblencs were preparing for a tournament or analyzing an adjourned game. At some point, his face suddenly acquired an impudent look and he stated: "Let's try making mischief here!" And it was clear that Tal would now suggest a fantastic, mind-boggling variation with multiple lines and sacrifices. If the combination was found to have a hole in it, he would get upset like a child, his lower lip would hang out, and he would say: "What a shame, the mischief doesn't work." And he was also mad about blitz, because in blitz he could make mischief all over the place.

His sudden rise to the chess throne was viewed by many as incomprehensible, inexplicable, totally illogical debauchery. His play was refuted, his combinations were proved to be incorrect, even suicidal. But all that happened later, after the game, after his opponents had been caught in a mating trap or otherwise found that their position was hopeless. Subsequently, they stopped refuting his play and came to accept his approach as a matter of course, as a cold fact. However, the new generation of players countered with a passionless pragmatic style, deliberately rejecting the "mischief" polemics that he proposed. Father had to change, he was forced to accept this cold pragmatism in order to hurt his opponents with their own weapons. People started to say that Tal had grown up. Or the opposite, that he had grown heavy and weary. Well, he always stayed true to his great self. Maybe he was more thoughtful. And if his opponent swallowed the hook that he had thrown them during the game he would drag an amazingly beautiful fish to the shore — and this gave him indescribable joy. I think that the number of best game prizes that he won, or prizes for the most beautiful combination, would be worthy of the Guinness Book of Records.

If a man leaves his home and heads for a romantic or business meeting, even a downpour won't stop him. He'll put on a raincoat or open up an umbrella. He is fully aware that he cannot stop the rain. Yet he has a choice – to wait for the rain to stop under a shop canopy, to return home or to outwit the rain with his umbrella and continue on his journey. To wait or return home means to be late, to disappoint the hopes of the person waiting for him. In other words, he will lose. My father didn't like to lose. For him, his pains were that same inevitable rain that he tried to outwit with this "medical umbrella". I shudder to think at the amount of medicine he consumed in his entire life! He was like a racing car rushing to the finishing line with a large number of faults from many years of use when there was never time to carry out repairs. In such cases, the car is patched up while in motion without any reduction in speed. Inevitably, the time will come when everything breaks down at the same time. My father's life was just that desperate race, and one day his body, his "car", gave up.

Some people accused Gelya of allowing him to drink, smoke and live in that mad rhythm, saying that she should have held him back, kept watch over him, and sent him to sanatoriums and hospitals. Well, those people weren't very smart, and they didn't know either my father or Gelya. My father would never have agreed to any restrictions on his personal freedom – that would have humiliated him, it would have knocked the pedestal of a winner from underneath him, and not to be a winner for him was no different from death. Gelya is a wonderful woman who understood my father, responsible for an achievement that no other woman would have managed – she lived with my father in *his* rhythm, on *his* terms – those that were essential for him.

I have nothing but admiration for her! I don't know anybody other than Gelya who could keep up with my father's pace, who could hold on to him like a racing horse over a distance. Despite all her love for my father, my mother never achieved that.

I attempted to "compete" with him a couple of times – but in vain... I remember once, I think it was in 1978, my father suggested I go with him to Leningrad (I think it was Leningrad but it may have been Moscow, I don't have my father's memory) to the USSR team championships. I was pleased – first, because I was travelling with my father, and secondly, because it gave me the chance to take my mind off my studies and my problems. We took a room in a hotel together and I joined in with his mad pace straight away. We would get up at six-thirty, grab a bite to eat in our room left over from the previous night's dinner, knock back a small brandy, and then he would analyze the previous day's game and prepare for that day's. A thick haze of cigarette smoke. My dad, hunched over the board, would mutter something and then make rapid piece movements. A cigarette in his mouth like a part of his facial structure – forehead, eyes, nose, mouth, cigarette. As he finished one he would automatically reach for another. Then his game, then lunch-cum-dinner with more brandy, and then time with friends – in our hotel room or at their place.

Then more alcohol, although not necessarily brandy, constant questions, my father's elegant and always amusing replies. He could never give a simple 'yes' or 'no' answer. He had to make a smart joke. Most people were delighted at him. They would specially ask him questions in the hope of hearing a witty, paradoxical or aphoristic answer. Replying, father would look deeply at his counterparty, as though searching in his eyes for an assessment of the reply he had just given. But some conversation partners find this a burden, and there were people who said that talking with Tal was exhausting. My father soon got bored by such people.

After it had all finished, in the dead of night, either we would see people off in a car or they would see us off. And then another six-thirty rise... "Goosevich, open the fridge. What's left over from our royal feast?"

Don't forget that this was during one of the peaks in his chess career...

Tal's chess career can be largely explained by his purely human traits. Trying to understand the lulls in his form, the reasons for his meteoric rise and equally short stay on the chess throne, many people make reference to his health. Of course, that has been important, but it is not the decisive factor. Chess today, just like any other human activity, requires total commitment to achieve success as the very top. Has Tal committed himself fully to chess, leaving nothing behind? I don't think so. An immensely gifted person all-round, an epicurean by nature, he hasn't wanted to forgo the many joys of life even for chess, even though there is no doubting Tal's fantastic love for the game. Nobody in the history of chess became world champion as early as Tal. His huge talent carried him to the very top in record time. In order to repeat that path, he would have had to spill much blood and sweat. Tal couldn't do that and probably didn't want to. Spending his entire life in an atmosphere of his fans' endless and total admiration and devotion, Tal was used to triumphs, but to immediate ones. To prepare for success gradually, years on end, in the quiet of a study-room, that isn't for Tal. On the contrary, dashing off to another city to play a blitz tournament in the very midst of preparing for a critical competition, waiting in the airport for three hours, grabbing the first available taxi, turning up at the tournament hall to the excited greetings of fans almost an hour late and, having triumphantly taken first place, rushing back to Riga – that's Tal in a nutshell. Outgoing, generous with his friendship, arty, it sometimes seems that he gains more pleasure from press-conferences after winning a tournament than from the tournament itself. It's not enough for Tal to come first, he has to take first place in style; it's not enough for him to win a game, he needs to have captured at least half of his opponent's pieces. Napoleon once lectured his marshals: "You cannot achieve success if you punch with each finger individually, you have to clench them into a fist." Tal hasn't concentrated all of his amazing talent into a single activity, to do that he would have to give up everything else. But in that case he wouldn't be Tal. His chess career isn't pre-programmed, it's vacillating, unstable, unpredictable...

N. Borisov, *64*, 1980

I don't have a weak constitution, but after three days I realized I had to stop. On day four I said to him: "Dad, forgive me, but I'm really busy, I'm missing my studies, Mum is on her own and Nadia's waiting for me." "It's a real shame, Goosenysh, that you're leaving me alone," he replied. "I hoped that we could spend a great couple of weeks."

Were he to suggest today spending not a couple of weeks with him in his hotel room but the rest of my life I would consider it the height of happiness. I would stick with him like a loyal dog, would breath his cigarette smoke, would stay up with him for several nights on end, would pretend that I understood when he showed me how he "made mischief" in the King's Indian the day before, I would even smoke as much as him and drink as much as well, and I would fall asleep totally exhausted, like him, in the armchair in the hotel lobby.

No, I'm lying – I wouldn't keep up, I don't have the strength. I would stop on day three... And now he'll never ask me again... At least, not in *this* life...

My mother Genya Lev and my father Boris Landau

Me and my mother

My parents still performing in 1982

Gera with my parents

With Tal's mother Ida

The day we got married

The crowd at Riga train station comes to greet the new world champion!

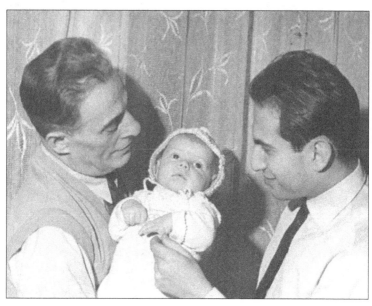

Robert, Misha and Gera

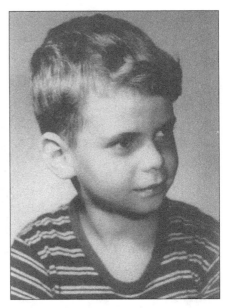

Gera

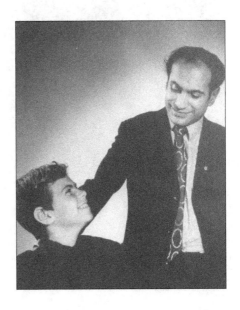

Me and my two husbands, Joe and Misha

Gera with Genna Sosonko, Tal Memorial, Moscow, 2008
(photo provided by Genna Sosonko)

CHAPTER 3

Sally Again

In some families, the birth of a first child becomes a turning point in the relations between the parents. They kind of "grow up". Once errant daddies sit at home, and if they allow themselves to go out, then only with the baby. A full maternal instinct blossoms in party girls, they wise up, the child replaces the husband with all his jokes and tomfoolery as the mother's main interest, and the parents reach a practical and dynamic equilibrium that makes the family function together as a unit.

However, in other families the model is quite different: the wife only nominally considers herself to be a mother. The child is a burden and the wife is afraid of missing out on partying before her youth evaporates. She begins to resent her husband, who, she thinks (and in some cases she is right), has dumped all of his parental responsibilities on her and continues to live life to the full. Further, if the wife is genetically a sloth and useless at everything, family life soon turns into Hell, consisting of piles of unwashed clothes and nappies (in those days, we Soviet people had never heard of disposables), dirty dishes, slapdash and cold meals. And among all of that, an until recently pretty woman who has let herself go, scruffy and forever wearing a dressing gown, bustles about here and there. Arguments in this situation are inevitable, and the husband either quietly develops a drink problem or finds himself consolation on the side.

In our family, Gera's birth led to a third scenario. I didn't immediately feel that I was a full mother. At first, my priority was for Misha to develop a father's feelings. I thought that Gera would "magnetize" Misha to himself, and, logically, to me, too. However, Misha didn't change. Gera, I repeat, appealed to him from time to time as an amusing toy that had arisen out of nowhere, like a sideline that appears during a chess game that has to be reckoned with but which doesn't warrant a piece sacrifice. Simply, the world chess champion had gained a son. Gera, Bulochka, Goose... And his Saska had become the queen mother... That is just what Misha said to me: "Saska! Now you are not simply my queen, you are my queen mother!"

As for me, after Gera was born my genetic germophobia morphed into true paranoia. I would chase away every fly, every speck of dust. I wouldn't sleep at night, waiting for Gerochka to wet himself in order to change his nappy immediately. I wouldn't take my eyes off the clock so that I wouldn't start feeding him late. At the same time, I not only regained my previous form but, it seemed to me, I gained something new, which transformed me from a young lass into an alluring lady. I managed to view myself frequently enough in the mirror and was pleased to see polished changes. I didn't demand that Misha constantly spend time with our son. I quickly realized that such demands were useless. Sometimes he would pick up Bulochka in his arms, engage him in baby talk, kiss him on the bottom, sniff him from head to toe, put him back in his cot and immediate return to his own world, again becoming the mysterious genius Tal for whom the rest of the world ceased to exist, who lived and thought in a parallel universe of black and white squares where he had no equal, where victory was natural and essential, where defeat was met with astonishment, like a runner who suddenly tripped up having broken out far in front of the pack, as a result of which he is caught and overtaken.

I felt upset by one thing: why Misha, calling me a queen, actually treating me at certain times like a queen, receiving from me everything that a beloved husband could receive, dissolving inside me to the maximum like a beloved husband could dissolve inside his beloved wife (and I say this with full justification, because Misha was incapable of lying in both his every-day and intimate life), why, despite all this, did he entertain other women who weren't queens and whom he didn't consider queens? I gained no comfort from his clumsy explanations. Nor was I convinced by Ida's smart arguments that Mishanka was from another world and that I shouldn't attach any importance to the amusements of a genius, for whom I would always remain the only woman; that to lose me would be a disaster for Misha that would wreck his chess career. I would listen, nod my head, but I foresaw that my jealousy, my selfish feminine nature, would sooner or later break the vicious circle, although I sincerely prayed to God that this would happen as late as possible, because I was afraid of it and didn't want it to happen. Ultimately, it did.

It's not easy to become world chess champion, but it's even harder to defend this esteemed title... How come Tal played so insipidly and with such uncertainty this year?!

I think that, above all, he underestimated Botvinnik. Further, Tal didn't prepare theory very well and, moreover, he wasn't in great physical shape. In the majority of games, once play reached a fifth hour Tal tired and frequently made decisive mistakes.

...Very few people expected Botvinnik to win, and Tal himself played too carelessly in the first half of the match. I think that the results of games three and seven were key to the match. Not only because Botvinnik won them, but because he countered Tal's aggressive play with sharp play of his own. After Tal managed to win game eight, he made what in my view was a big psychological and tactical blunder. Even though Tal had been ill for several

days, he played game nine in too gung-ho a fashion, chose a very risky variation and was naturally punished. As we saw, that defeat impacted Tal significantly, and this explains his uncertain play in the final two games...

...What else can I say about Tal? He fought stubbornly until the last minute and lost sportingly. It's important to note that he wasn't in good form and he lacks experience, especially in the endgame. However, possessing an immense talent Tal will surely fix his weaknesses. Who knows, maybe he will win the candidates tournament?

Gideon Stahlberg, Chief Arbiter of the return match, *Pravda*, 13 May 1961

After the return match, Misha was placed in the Republican Hospital. Obviously, he had his own room with all the appropriate privileges. One day when I went to see him, I found a solid-looking middle-aged man with a crew cut him in his room. They were playing chess. Misha introduced us. I won't name him in this book. Why? Let's say that he was a high-up government official... I will call him "the Minister"... Let that be his name here.

He rose, kissed my hand, said he was very pleased to meet me, and I immediately made a note that he was looking at me not only as Mikhail Tal's wife... Women always sense these things. I knew that men liked me, I even mentioned it to Misha: "You know that men stare at me?" "Of course!" he replied. "I even know why. You are beautiful, pure, remarkable, and your kindness seeps through. Why shouldn't they fall for you?"

"Yeah, true, why shouldn't they fall for me?" I asked myself rather immodestly. "I'm pretty, nicely shaped, kind... And on top of all that I'm Mikhail Tal's wife... I've never done anything bad to anyone in my life."

I don't feel envy for anybody, or if I do envy somebody, then it's people like Barbara Streisand or Luciano Pavarotti... I'm envious of people's talent, of their health... At the very least because all my life I have suffered monstrous headaches that drove not only me up the wall but Misha too, because he didn't know how to help me.

They played some more chess, then we sat together, chatted for a while, and as I got up to leave for home he also got up. A car was waiting for him outside the hospital. He drove me home, opened the passenger door and helped me out of the car. Then he suddenly asked: "May I kiss you on the cheek?" "Sure," I answered.

That day, I cross-examined Robert about him. It turned out that he was not only a Minister but also a leading chess official. And had recently got divorced...

Fast forwarding, I can say that Robert, being a practical person, soon began to use my "female charm" to get closer to the Minister. At Robert's behest, I got the Minister to obtain all the medicine that Misha needed, and to provide sanitarium stays. Thanks to him, we found a job for Yasha. I remember once calling the Minister's office, I can't remember what for, and his secretary Maria answered: "He's not here right now. He has a message for you that he will be waiting for you in his office in two hours." He received me very earnestly, his secretary made us coffee, and as I got up to leave he told me: "You know, Sally, the doors of my office are always open for you. I will carry out any request you have with the greatest of pleasure." A few days later, I showed up again at his office, and Maria said to me: "He has a totally different mood when you come to visit. He really brightens up."

Then I began to encounter him on the street, too. At first, I assumed that this happened by chance. But I soon realized that this wasn't the case. I would head for home after rehearsals and a car would draw up next to me. This elegant Minister would emerge from the car, kiss my hand, tell me that he'd been thinking about me all day and (ha ha!) say that it was so lovely to encounter me unexpectedly. He would invite me to coffee at a cafe, buy me flowers and complain every time: "Why do you never invite me to your shows? The whole of Riga is talking about Sally the actress!"

I realized that I was only hearing the "expected" compliment from him, but I have to admit that I enjoyed it. It was further confirmation that I had made the right choice to continue my career, especially with Misha insisting that I give up the theater. Basically, it had become abundantly clear that the Minister was showering me with attention not only as Mikhail Tal's wife. This intrigued my female nature. I certainly wasn't indifferent to the fact that such an interesting, quite remarkable "mature" man (he later turned out to be sixteen years older than me) was courting me, but the only thought that I had at the time was the simple fact that he found me attractive. It didn't occur to me for one second that it would be thanks to his involvement that I would break the vicious circle that had caught me.

Meanwhile, Misha was discharged from hospital without any specific diagnosis and he left for Moscow to play in a tournament.

Sometime later, Ida told me that Misha had found a new admirer, that she was a film actress, a woman of remarkable beauty who was madly in love with chess, and that she was passionate about Misha. Ida told me all this with some sort of inexplicable delight, but she again asked me not to pay serious attention to it, as Tal needed to have admirers and this was perfectly normal. I didn't have to make much of an effort to find confirmation of Ida's words.

I won't say anything about this lady now — good or bad. I have no idea about her life now. But at the time I took the bit between my teeth. My previous "jealousies" and suspicions were nothing compared with what I now experienced. I hated L. from a distance. I don't consider it ethical or purposeful to give her name today. I also felt sorry for myself: she was beautiful, she was talented, she was this and that. And who was I? Cinderella? Zamarashka[16]? Limping Asya[17]? I would cry, pour myself a stiff drink, get angry, think of revenge, yet during my phone calls with Misha I never asked him a single question about L.. And he, naturally, said nothing to me, except that he missed me and Bulochka, and that he was desperate to see us again. Now I realize that Misha didn't try to hide anything from me, and didn't intend to deceive me. He simply believed his actions to be perfectly normal, like a sideline that would suddenly appear in a game of chess.

I even think that sometimes he made no distinction between life and chess. Chess was his life, these wooden pieces were enlivened by his talent and imagination and began to resemble people, while the people around him were chess pieces moving along their allocated squares, files and diagonals, *who could be sacrificed*, who defended and attacked, and who were meant to lead him to victory, because nothing else was possible. Therefore, any human "chess piece" suddenly displaying its independence genuinely astonished Misha. When I (much later) told him that

---

[16] A character in a Russian story by Ivan Khudyakov similar to Cinderella

[17] The country-dwelling heroine of a film by Andrei Konchalovsky who is beaten by her driver boy-friend from whom she is expecting a child yet puts up with that and rejects the marriage offer from a city-dwelling middle-aged man who is madly in love with her

he had betrayed me and exchanged me, he simply smiled and said: "Saska! You are my main and most wonderful piece. It's wrong to exchange such pieces! Ask Gufeld. He says that to exchange Sally is like exchanging the dark-squared bishop in a King's Indian!"

I was too young and self-centered to understand all this. But even today, though I am now of a mature age, I can affirm with absolute certainty: even if I had understood it, my nature and my very being would never have accepted such a state of affairs. I wasn't fated to feel that I was person number two in life. One set of circumstances had brought me and Misha together, and now another set of circumstances led to a rupture in our relationship. At first, it seemed like a minor fracture. There was still the chance for him to take a step towards me and for me to take a step towards him, but the process eventually became irreversible, depending on neither of us. Early on, it seemed that we could cross the water that had come between us by swimming, then by boat, but then we were so far away that we could barely make each other out, and eventually we stopped even hearing each other. After that, the only communication possible was by phone, and finally, we needed an aircraft in order to visit each other.

However, the longer the distance between us, the more painfully we realized that we were on opposite ends of an umbilical cord, one that stretched endlessly but which nobody was ready to cut. And nothing could be done to improve the situation, all that remained was the pain from taking note of it. And the pain-killing consolation: "my Saska"... "my Misha"... "She's with somebody else, but nevertheless with me"... "He's with somebody else, but nevertheless with me".

If that wasn't bad enough, Robert was arrested in 1962 and sent to prison – I don't know and don't care if he was guilty.

This was part of the notorious Rozenblum case – Rozenblum was the head of commerce in Latvia. Misha wasn't in Riga at the time. The doorbell rang one morning. Robert opened the door, then ran into my room, and informed me somewhat incoherently that he was being arrested. The case was widely reported. Robert risked a long sentence, but in the end spent about a year and a half in prison. Things got tougher at home, as Robert provided for the entire family. Now I had to maintain little Gera, Ida and the apartment. I began to sell all the expensive clothes that Misha had brought us. We had no savings at the time: Robert was incapable of putting money away. He was too charitable and generous for that. When friends and colleagues emigrated from the USSR he would personally pack their crates of belongings, paid for the baggage and for the containers with furniture (furniture made in Riga!), and sometimes even bought their tickets. Several years later, he said to me in passing: "If those people had returned at least some of that money I would be a millionaire." Meanwhile, I earned a meagre 120 roubles per month, so I sold off just about everything I could find.

I remember in particular one upsetting episode during those days. Misha played in Cuba at the Capablanca memorial in August - September 1964. His fee was paid in certificates – and he bought L. an Astrakhan lambswool coat with it ("well-wishers" were vigilant as usual and immediately told me about this). After returning from Cuba, Misha spent several days in Riga. The entire time he was hyper-active, absent minded, and endlessly phoned Moscow. I obviously guessed whom he was calling. Anybody could see that he was in a state of infatuation, to put it mildly. I tried to appear cold and nonchalant, though I found this quite difficult to maintain. He languished for several days in Riga and then flew to Moscow. And I knew damned well whom he went to see.

I also knew that, thanks to L., he had got in with a group of well-known film actors: Rybnikov, Larionova, some others, too. They would meet up every day, and Misha spent all the money that he had on them. I don't want to say anything negative about anybody. I wouldn't say that they were taking him to the cleaners: Misha gained pleasure from spending the money, as well as from showing off in front of L.. However, the facts are undeniable: I was selling our clothes in Riga to make ends meet, while in Moscow Misha was giving L. expensive presents that he bought without a moment's thought.

Both my mental and financial states were dreadful. I invited my father over from Vilnius. He showed up and told me: "Misha is your husband, and he's a genius. You need to show understanding and take a sensible approach. Don't provoke him into a divorce, but don't wait for him to return to you. Begin an independent life again. You're also a singer. I'll help you both as a father and as the director of the Vilnius Entertainment Orchestra. Gerochka can live in Vilnius with me and your mother for now, and then we'll see. But please don't divorce Misha. Everything will come out in the wash."

I wasn't planning on divorcing Misha, and certainly didn't want to get remarried. I needed to think about myself and my child. I knew that here nobody would help me, not even the Minister, who was still madly in love with me, and to whom, following his persistence, I eventually gave myself, exhausted, frustrated and lonely.

That's life... Two key factors throw a woman into the vortex of infidelity: first, adultery by her beloved husband (*beloved*, because if you do not love him then you become indifferent to him and all his "playing away", and you don't feel that he has betrayed you or committed an offense against you), and then, after that, the moral emptiness and total vulnerability that you feel. An emotional woman is capable of anything in this case. Women who love adventures often simply jump at circumstances that appear by chance. But if a smart, tactful man who loves her appears then a betrayed woman takes a fateful decision in favor of that man, and after a while she either truly becomes passionate about him or else convinces herself that she is.

Misha remained as though behind a curtain, and for ages I didn't want to open it. He felt hurt, and I think that my relationship with the Minister played a role in his ending his lengthy affair with L..

I think that my affair wounded him hard, though I swear I had no such intention. The Minister and I didn't publicize our liaisons, but nor did we hide them, at least for a while. He was domineering but loved me dearly. Add to this his standing in Latvia, his age, and you will realize the background to his quite abnormal jealousy towards me. His "team" had me under surveillance twenty-four hours a day. They would photograph me whenever I entered a hotel and photograph me again whenever I exited it. I couldn't go to a restaurant or the cinema unnoticed. I would walk along the street and look behind my back, like a spy in a detective film. The Minister's driver would stop Gera in the street and ask, "where's Mummy?" or "who phoned Mummy?" The Minister had a sort of mental illness when it came to me. He would phone Misha's mother and ask where I was. And if Ida replied, for example, that I was in the bathroom, he would call back fifteen minutes later and ask why I was taking so long.

Did I love him? Probably, yes... And I was afraid of him. Although I realized that he would never do anything nasty to me. His jealousy and suspiciousness were not only down to his senior professional standing, and not only to his domineering nature, but above all because he was terrified of losing me. Our relations were outrageous – scandalous – in the eyes of the entire population of Riga. The Minister was unable to evade the communist hypocrisy and puritanism. He had become a "stain" on the Latvian Central Committee of the Communist Party. They wagged their fingers at him. They ordered him to appear at the Central Committee, where they told him: "You won't remain a member of the Central Committee or a Minister. You will be a nobody if you don't break this liaison that blackens you as a Communist. Your 'lady' is the official wife of Mikhail Tal." He told me this himself. He proposed that I divorce Misha and marry him, but this didn't make sense for me – much as I was drawn to him, and despite everything he had done for me, I realized that our marriage would not be a happy one, because we were from, as it were, different teams. He was of an upper caste, an ethnic Latvian, a Central Committee member, while I was a Jewish actress from an unremarkable family, and with no pedigree to speak of. I was fine to keep things as they were. I'll say more – I was pretty comfortable with those arrangements.

He was further incensed by the fact that I remained a totally independent woman. I was hired through a competitive recruitment process by the Vilnius Jazz Orchestra and quickly became its leading soloist. We began a tour throughout the USSR. I started to earn a decent salary, and my only problem was what to do with Gera. As we left to perform in Soviet Asia, he remained with Ida, but Ida then got seriously ill, and her friend, who worked in a sanatorium for orphans, took in Gera.

Gera spent three hated months in the sanatorium. Meanwhile, I had bad luck of my own. I needed an urgent operation in Ashgabat, Turkmenia. There I was lying in the hospital, it was forty degrees Celsius outside, electric fans, draughts. In the post-op period I caught pneumonia in both my lungs and very nearly died.

I flew to Riga as soon as I recovered. My heart bled when I came to visit Gerochka in the sanatorium, when I saw him with all his hair shaved off, dressed in what looked like prisoner's grey overalls. I burst into tears, he grabbed hold of me and begged me to take him away. So I did. Then the three of us — my mother, Gera and I — spent a couple of months on the Black Sea, and after that my mother took Gera to her home in Vilnius. During our holiday in the South, I was introduced to Eddie Rosner, the famous jazz artist. He listened to me sing and invited me to join his equally famous orchestra. So I began to tour with Rosner.

As I said earlier, I maintained very warm relations with Ida. Like I was her daughter. Indeed, she would always address me as "my daughter". Whenever I could, I would send money from my travels to Riga. Robert had by now been released from prison. He was horrified at learning of Misha's affair with L.. And all the suspicion and lack of trust that he experienced in relation to me before his arrest fell away in an instant. He embraced me with fatherly love and tenderness and retained this attitude towards me until he died.

During breaks between our tours, I would return to Vilnius. Even when I was there, the Minister would continue to keep tabs on me. Sometimes he would phone, sometimes his secretary, or even his driver: where am I, who am I with, what am I doing, where have I been? He turned up in Vilnius himself quite a lot. He would bring presents for me, my parents, Gera. He would appear in the doorway with wrapped up parcels in one hand and would extend his other hand to Gera, saying "Hello, son!" In return, Gera would wave a bare foot at him and reply: "I have a daddy, and I'm his son. Who are you?" Gera couldn't stand him. Many years later, already in emigration, Gera and I were sitting in a cafe in Berlin when he said to me: "I will tell you this for the first and only time in my life. I love you madly and always have done. I couldn't bear it when anybody else touched you or even simply greeted you. That's how much I loved you. I will never tell you this again."

Meanwhile, the Minister took a dislike to Misha, to put it mildly. Once he showed up in Vilnius with a female colleague when I was absent and spent the whole evening cross-examining mother about whether I planned to return to Misha. I never cease to be surprised at such men! Their selfishness is incomparable! They always want to keep what they have! They can never accept losing anything.

The Communists eventually broke my Minister's resistance and forced him to marry the daughter of a well-known party functionary in order to restore party disciple. Say what you will, but their method of tying up their own people by hand and foot was practiced to perfection.

Now, the Minister being once again married, secretly maintained relations with me, and worried most of all that I would go back to Misha. Moreover, after a while he even found me a separate apartment in Riga, so that he would be able to keep constant watch over me. My father was genuinely worried that one of those days a car would run me over in the street, as "Mrs. Minister" was aware of our liaisons and, naturally, wasn't happy about them. Moreover, this cast a shadow over her father. Dad even said to me: "You need to find a way to end it all yourself, otherwise the KGB will suddenly make you disappear. As Stalin used to say, 'no person – no problem'."

However, I naturally didn't think about this and assigned no importance to my father's words – I just stuck my head in the sands and went with the flow. *Que sera sera.*

Misha behaved the same as always. He often phoned Ida and asked after me and Gera, saying that he would soon be back in Riga and missed us. When I visited Gorky Street he would

phone me, tell me he was in love with me, that there was nobody
better than me, that he was dying to get back to Riga. But not
a word about L.. It was as though she didn't exist. And I never
let on that I was in some ways interested in this story of his.
On occasions, he arrived back at the apartment for a couple of
days, but I was never there. Ida, despite all her love for Misha,
would complain every time from the very first day of his visits:
"My God, I hope he leaves soon! This mad house has to stop!
Endless pioneers! Endless journalists! The apartment is thick
with smoke!"

Misha knew about my Minister, but he never asked me about
him – he would try to get information out of Ida. He found it
impossible to imagine his "Saska" belonging to anybody else.
One of his friends told me in chess style: "Sally! Once Misha
fully realized that you had this Minister he acted as though he
had just blundered a piece without understanding how he did it.
And he won't forgive either himself or you for this 'blunder'."
So now we were quits – I couldn't forgive him for L.. Later,
I became relaxed about his affairs, as though they weren't
important, although all this was still unpleasant. L. even now
provokes a storm of negative emotions in me. I realize that all
this happened a very long time ago, but I can't stop myself.

Just imagine my horror when Ida told me: "My daughter,
Misha wants to bring L. to Riga. He wants to introduce her to
us, and to you above all. You have to understand his state of
mind. After all, you're smart. We should simply greet her as one
of Misha's really good friends."

"I understand," I replied. "I'll do everything I can to make
Misha happy."

So they arrived. Misha's "really good friend" was put up at
Aunty Hanna's place (Ida's sister). Actually, a novel could have
been written about Aunty Hanna's life. While in Paris, Aunty

Hanna married a talented French engineer who one fine day got infected with the idea of moving to the USSR to selflessly help the Soviet people build communism (quite a number of western intellectuals fell victim to this idea). His Soviet venture ended typically: at the end of the 1930s he was arrested as a foreign spy and shot, while Aunty Hanna spent seven years in prison as the wife of an "enemy of the people".

The very evening when L. arrived in Riga, Misha brought her round to Gorky Street. He acted as though nothing had happened – he was loving and tender towards me, told jokes and asked me to tell L. funny episodes from our trip to Curacao. L. seemed astonished at such a warm welcome. I enquired about her work, her parents, her friends. Misha sat me down at the piano. I played it and sang, and he accompanied me as a backing vocalist. Misha was happy. It seemed to me that he was really enjoying this scenario that he had contrived. He reminded me of a theater director who had correctly allocated the right roles in his play to the right actors. Then it was time for Misha to accompany L. to Aunty Hanna's place. I was sure that he wouldn't return, but Ida told me: "If Mishanka returns then we have won." Misha did indeed return, and he and I spent un unforgettable night together. But Ida had got it wrong – "we" hadn't won. The next day, he flew back to Moscow with L.. When he then came to Riga with L. a second time, it was me and Gerochka who were packed off to Aunty Hanna's – there was nowhere else to put us.

I can't imagine who would have envied me. The situation had become tense. One day, when I was staying with Ida between tours, Misha showed up unexpectedly. That evening, when we were all at home, the Minister suddenly phoned and asked for me. Misha, naturally, guessed from my confused face who was calling and left the room. The Minister spent ages declaring his love for me and then said: "Tell me that you love me." "Look, you know that," I replied, trying to avoid his request. I paused and then hung up. Misha then re-appeared in the room and gave me a questioning look. I couldn't think of anything more sensible to say than, "it was a wrong number." Misha smiled somewhat artlessly and said: "I think I've got the wrong number."

Right then I wished that L. would disappear from his life, that the Minister would disappear from mine, and that Misha and I would remain as a couple. Perhaps he had the same thought... However, the fracture that had appeared between us had already turned into a chasm, and by then was probably unsurmountable.

Meanwhile, Misha's affair with L. had started to lead to somewhat unpleasant consequences. Misha hid nothing from anybody, but even if he had tried to he would have been unlikely to succeed – Mikhail Tal was too much of a celebrity in those days. One day, in early 1964, Tal was summoned to the Central Committee and told: "Mikhail Nekhemyevich, you are famous throughout the world, but you live in the Soviet Union, so you are a Soviet person. You have a wife, a child, and everybody in the world, even in the West, is gossiping about the fact that you have a mistress. You could even call her an official mistress. Please make your mind up. Either live with your wife and forget your mistress, or, if you must, divorce your wife and make an honest woman out of your mistress. Obviously, that is a less desirable outcome, but we will treat you with understanding." Misha, as he himself told me later, replied curtly that it had nothing to do with them and that he would continue to live as he pleased. "Well, you can make your own decisions," the officials told him. He left the meeting effectively banned from travelling to tournaments abroad – it was soon made clear to him that he would not be going to the next interzonal (Amsterdam, May - June 1964).

I found out about this from Ida, and she asked me to come round and discuss what to do. I said that I would do absolutely all that was in my power... If, of course, I had any influence at all. Ida hinted that it might be a good idea to involve the Minister. I promised to ask, although as I'm sure you appreciate I didn't want to involve him. Ida asked me to write a letter to the Central Committee, saying that Misha wasn't at all guilty, that he was a wonderful husband and father, that I was a bad wife, that it was me who had been long unfaithful to him, and that I didn't want to live with him in any case. It was hard to make myself write such a letter, but I convinced myself to do it: if the letter would help Misha I would write it whatever it cost me. I wrote the letter and we sent it to the Central Committee. Misha was summoned to the committee again and they showed him the letter... I can only imagine what he was going through reading my "confession". They told him that my letter was insufficient, and if he wanted to continue to date L. then he would have to divorce me. Actually, they had a real laugh at him – they told him that usually the letters from wives that they received said the opposite, that the wives asked for their errant husbands to be punished, to be thrown out of the party and banned from travelling abroad. This was the first time they had received a letter from a wife defending her husband after bad behavior, and they joked they would frame it and hang it on the wall.

Misha returned to Riga. He was very fretful and I had never seen him so confused either before or since. For the first time, he sensed that he was dependent on circumstances that in a normal society would have no impact whatsoever on his participation in the interzonal, or on his private life at all. However, Ida invented a crazy move, in fact not so much a move as an entire combination! In the spirit of Misha's elaborate tricks, I (and not Misha!) would submit a petition to the district court to divorce

my husband Mikhail Tal, and after, on that basis, he was allowed
to play at the interzonal, I would withdraw my petition(!).
"Mum!" I said (despite everything that had happened I called
Ida Mum, as I loved her and treated her like a mother). "I'm
ready to do anything for Misha. If I have to submit a petition
then I will, but how can I withdraw it? If he loves that woman, if
he wants to live with her, a divorce will untie his hands." "No,"
she replied. "That's the whole point. Mishanka doesn't need
any of this, and he has no plans to divorce you. You'll see, it will
all work out in the end."

We went to the court together with Misha. I think that Robert
was the most nervous. Firstly, he objected to the relationship
with L., and secondly, he was very worried about Gera. "You
guys don't think about the child," he said, "but Gera senses all
of this. You're turning him into a cripple." After our petition
was accepted, Misha hugged me and said: "Thank you, Saska.
Believe me, it's going to be fine for all of us. Whatever happens,
I will never forget this my entire life."

An announcement of our impending divorce soon appeared
in a Riga newspaper with a report *Sally Landau has petitioned to
divorce Mikhail Tal*. The announcement was sent to the Central
Committee, and Misha got to play at the interzonal. Actually,
I'm not sure that it was this step that settled the issue in Misha's
favor. I think that the Minister's intervention was crucial –
naturally, I had asked him to help. I remember him frowning
and saying: "I will try to resolve this, but for your sake, not for
his." And once Misha had left for the tournament Ida forced me
to withdraw the petition.

I still to this day cannot understand how, with all my pride
and independence, I forced myself to write that letter, and why,
not wanting a divorce, I first filed for one and then withdrew
my petition. Clearly, I was under the sway of the Tal family, to

which, despite everything, I was strongly tied. But most probably, my actions were the result of Misha's incredibly powerful and unearthly chemistry.

I'm no strong chess player, to put it mildly. I couldn't get passionate about chess, and, unlike many "chess wives", I could never pretend to have a good knowledge of the game.

Misha once woke me up at night and said: "Saska, how about I teach you chess?" He placed a board right on the bed, stood the pieces in their places and right until morning explained how the rook moved, how the queen moved, and so on. But if I sort of mastered the rules of how pieces moved along ranks, files and diagonals (though I never caught the point of such moves), the knight totally confused me. By morning, even the stubborn Tal chucked the board off the bed and exclaimed: "I give up on you! It's up to you. Of all the chess pieces, you are the most valuable and the most universal. When my beautiful queen dominates the entire board and all the other pieces admire her and look at her in fright, I say to myself. That's not any old queen. That's my queen Saska!"

I understand nothing about chess, but I know a thing or two about the logic of human behavior. I think I do, anyway. And yet all of Misha's sorties, his crazy attacks and unexpected retreats, his frenzied bursts of tenderness and love, which were suddenly followed by unexplained disappearances, remain to this day beyond my understanding.

I continued to work with Eddie Rosner, while Misha had his tournaments and his love affair with L.. One day, while I was on a tour in the Crimea, Ida called me from Riga and said that Misha had arrived there out of the blue. When he found out that I was in Yalta, he asked Ida to pack his suitcase and put his swimming trunks in it. Then he ordered a ticket to Simferopol and flew to Yalta. I should expect him.

Misha had fantastic intuition. And it proved right this time.

In Yalta, the "Tsar" (as the orchestra called Rosner) had been paying special attention to me. Misha acted as though nothing had happened, as though he had never known any L. and as though I had never known any Minister. He arrived in the role of a man missing his beloved lady. He bought me flowers (he always guessed well with flowers) and other presents. He enchanted the entire orchestra and made friends with the Tsar. The second evening of Misha's stay, the Tsar got up on stage with a chess set and announced: "Right now the phenomenal Sally Tal, whose husband the phenomenal chess genius Mikhail Tal is sitting in the audience, will perform for you." Upon Rosner's sign, Misha stood up and the audience gave him an ovation.

All those days that Misha spent in Yalta, he put on sumptuous lunches and dinners, and each time toasted me. Rosner once suggested drinking to the health of the chess king, whereupon Misha immediately interjected: "I am the ex-king, but my queen here will never have the prefix 'ex'." On the last day of his stay, he suddenly said: "Saska, I'm flying off tomorrow. I think that the Tsar has taken a liking to you. Watch out."

"Is that all that you wanted to tell me?" I asked.

"I have told you not all the words," he sang back.

I never figured out why Misha suddenly flew to Yalta.

He again disappeared into an unknown world. Sometime later, Rosner, in the presence of his wife, told me in a by-the-way fashion that L. had just appeared on TV, where she claimed in a confident manner that she considered herself to be Tal's wife and that they would soon marry. Thereupon, I wrote Tal a firm letter asking for a divorce. I said that I'd had enough of his lengthy "simultaneous display" with me and L., that I had done everything that Ida had asked of me, and that I did it exclusively for his sake. I added that this time he needed to be the initiator of the divorce so that I wouldn't become a laughing stock, that in doing so he would free both our hands and that it would bring us both relief. Misha's reply arrived rather quickly. This second letter, like his first, I still have in my possession.

When I am feeling really sick, I re-read Misha's letters. I try to adopt his mind-set from that period in order to understand him. I think that by the time he sent the second letter (the first being the one he sent from Yugoslavia that I mentioned in Chapter 1 of this book) clouds were already hanging over relations between him and L.. Maybe he was just frustrated, but didn't want to admit this to anybody, including to himself. Or maybe L. had started to hint that it wouldn't be a bad idea to put a ring on her finger.

At least, this is what I guessed from his letter. Still, he expressed quite clearly his attitude to me and to our futures, and I have no doubt about his sincerity. I repeat, he didn't know how to lie. Here is the letter:

Dear Saska!

At last, I have managed to drag myself away and find a little time to talk with my Ginger. I'm not very well – I've spent almost all my time clutching a hot water bottle...

Sallynka my darling, I really want you to come to Riga, there is lots we need to discuss. What happened [the fact that he and I didn't get back together in Yalta] – well, really that is only for historical records now...

My darling, I'm sure that my game is approaching the finale. Both players are openly experiencing much irritation with each other and I now have to hear frequently: "My God, what a fool I've been! I had a great life, I had my apartment, dresses, shoes, a beloved(!!) job, while you, you bloody this and bloody that, have taken away everything I had. It's time for me to think about myself."

OK, let her think what she wants, I'm not too bothered. Please understand, Sallynka, that everything sorts itself out in time, and that time is to our advantage – to yours, above all. I wanted to come to your concert, but this damned process [his kidney problem] has practically tied me to Riga for a long time to come. Yes, Saska, what was that nonsense about a TV report?! There was not and could not have been any such report. It's just that a correspondent in Kiev attempted to interview L., but I quickly pushed him away. And the report could not have existed for the simple reason that I didn't leave my hotel room for 17 days, apart from being taken to the tournament hall and sitting (on my own, obviously) behind the chess board. [Misha meant that L. would not have been interviewed except in his presence.] The closing ceremony wasn't broadcast on TV at all, and moreover, all the grandmasters at that moment in time were bachelors (or temporarily married, let's say enjoying themselves) [meaning that L. wasn't at the closing ceremony so she couldn't have been interviewed there, either]. When you come we can tell each other everything.

Sallynka, please be a little more careful with the Tsar. Do you remember, when you were still in the Crimea you predicted that this would happen [that Rosner would hit on me]? But if everything happens as you predicted, maybe you should think twice about pursuing a relationship with him. There's no need to increase your number of victories – nobody (including your Miska) doubts your infinite capabilities.

My darling, I really miss you and my beloved Bulochka. I really hope that my mother gets better so that he can come and live in Riga.

I kiss you tenderly, am waiting for your news, and above all to meet up with you. Regards to the subjects of the Powerful Rosner Tsardom. I kiss you again. Your Miska.

After reading this letter, I totally ceased to understand what was going on, and once again decided to go with the flow. Rosner had kept saying to me that he would organize me an apartment and registration in Moscow so that I could live there peacefully with Gera. Time went on, and neither apartment nor registration materialized. However, had he kept his promise, I had only a hazy idea of how life in Moscow would pan out, if only because I couldn't imagine who would remain with my son during our tours. I wasn't going to take him with me like a circus performer! At the same time, bringing my parents to Moscow was quite unrealistic.

I soon left Rosner's orchestra and returned to work at the Vilnius orchestra. Misha once again started to bombard me with phone calls. He would call from everywhere, and sometimes I could even make out L. bawling drunkenly in the background. I heard from a number of people that L. couldn't stop once she started to drink. I repeat, Misha was exceptionally generous. In those days, chess players' earnings were pretty decent, and he would return from his foreign trips with several suitcases packed with presents. L. would always meet him at the airport, and the key object of her attention was the luggage. Well, I have reason to believe that this is exactly what happened. I hope she forgives me if I'm wrong. I don't know what drove them to split up. Nobody shared the details of their scandalous finale, but some chess players and their wives told me that after a tournament he hid from her in the Hotel Moscow, that she went looking for him, badgered the entire hotel floor, and tried to break into Misha's room. It ended with Misha opening the door and chucking all the suitcases that he had brought with him into the corridor. After that, she disappeared from Misha's life. I don't know what happened to her after that... and I don't care.

I only worked briefly with the orchestra in Lithuania. I remember going on a trip to Leningrad. After one of the concerts there I returned to my hotel to encounter Misha waiting for me in the lobby. He had the demeanour of a guilty child who knew that he had misbehaved but who was sure to be forgiven.

He had flown in from Moscow unexpectedly, and I got worried that something had happened. "Saska!" he said, "don't worry! Everything's fine! I'm hungry, but the food's great in the Astoria[18], I've reserved a table for two there."

"You came here to have dinner with me, and to have breakfast with *her* in Moscow?" I asked.

"No," he replied with his disarming smile, "it's just that I have told you not all the words..."

We headed to the restaurant. A basket with beautiful flowers stood on the table. I got ready for yet another long conversation on a by now familiar subject. We ate mostly in silence for some time, just asking each other trivial questions now and then. The orchestra was terrible. Misha was going strong on the brandy and getting tipsier by the minute. Evidently, he needed to build up some bravura. Then, he suddenly asked me for a dance. "Misha," I said, "you mean to say she taught you to dance?" He turned all serious and said: "Ginger! You know that I don't like to cultivate old images. The only image that I like to cultivate is yours."

And he began to swear that his affair with L. was over forever, that the two of us resembled two ships that had crashed into each other and that the only way to save us was to help each other reach the port, that it was pointless trying to find the reasons for the crash, that we needed to mend the holes as quickly as

---

[18] Not to be confused with the Astoria restaurant in Riga

possible and continue our sea journey together. Oh, he knew how to speak convincingly, and I did believe his sincerity, but I told him that I was quite tired of this meaningless sailing, that I wanted to live peacefully on the shore *alone*. "Alone?" he asked as though deep in thought. "Is that all you care about?" I asked. "I don't want you to live alone. I want you to live with me." "Mishanka," I replied, "I loved you dearly and continue to love you, but everything's gone too far and it doesn't matter who was guilty. If you think that I was guilty then so be it. But I don't want to take my move back, because I don't want to be worrying about your next object of passion. We will remain close friends. We have a wonderful son." I couldn't stop myself any longer and burst into tears. Misha started to stroke me and tried to console me. "Misha, people are staring at as." "Let them be jealous," Misha replied.

He brought a bottle of brandy with him to his hotel room and begged me until two a.m. to forget everything and begin again. And much as I felt deep pain for him, for myself, for Gera, I told him: "Misha, I need to get some sleep. My rehearsals start tomorrow morning."

At this point, he had an awful seizure. He turned pale, sweat broke out all over his face, and once again I noticed this unworldly terror in his eyes that made him appear frightening. "I'm in excruciating pain," he barely spluttered. Alarmed, I ran into the corridor, awoke the concierge and asked him to call an ambulance. The ambulance arrived quickly. The medics glanced at Misha, at his unfinished bottle of brandy, exchanged knowing looks and got to work. A minute later, they injected Misha with Pantopon, after which he felt better. He smiled weakly, apologized to the doctors for taking up their time, and then said: "Forgive me, Saska. I have these problems. You know that." And he asked me to put my hand on his forehead. One of the doctors, filling in the form, asked: "Are you that very same Tal?" "Why, is there another Tal?" Misha retorted. "You need to check your kidneys," the doctor went on. "Pantopon is a dangerous substance." They remained for another ten minutes, took Misha's autograph and left.

The next morning, Misha flew to Moscow, and after that encounter we didn't see each other for a long period of time.

That September, Gerochka began school. And I changed employer again and joined the Riga Entertainment Orchestra. I had to solve the problem of Gera. Now I could no longer pass him around during my tours between my mother in Vilnius and Ida's sister Hanna, but nor could I fully leave him with Ida — she was seriously ill and her illness was progressing. My son and I moved back into the apartment on Gorky Street, which made Ida and Robert overjoyed. After the story with L. they had started to treat me especially nicely. Ida endlessly repeated that she would only die peacefully once she saw Misha and I together again. "You mustn't abandon Misha, my daughter," she would say. "You don't realize how much you mean to him."

Misha "attacked" me one further time after I returned from touring East Germany. I got off the train and saw Misha on the platform. He was wearing a suit and tie, with his usual bouquet of opulent flowers. He saw me and ran up, hugged me and triumphantly gave me the flowers. Actually, quite a few people had come to meet me off the train and were waiting on the platform, including the Minister's driver, looking sullen and standing aside. I kissed Misha and told him calmly: "Mishanka, I'm sorry, but people have come to meet me." And then I was whisked off to see the Minister.

Ida later told me that it was she who persuaded Misha to meet me with flowers at the station (until the very last minute she never lost hope that we would reconcile), that Misha had returned home extremely upset, and that he had said: "Murochka, I did all that you asked... Evidently, Saska never loved me."

Well, I don't know whether it was to get his own back on me, or a matter of his self-esteem, or a sincere passion of his, but Misha soon brought a second L. to the apartment. And so a totally peculiar period began that was quite impenetrable to anybody from the outside. Gera and I lived in one room, Misha and L. number two in the lounge, plus Ida, plus Robert, plus Yasha – all in the same apartment. L. number two was fairly young and very pretty. Oddly enough, though I intensely disliked L. number one, I was quite neutral about L. number two. Gera got on with her fine, called her "Aunty" and never asked me about her. I don't know whether he understood what was going on, or whether he was too little. I can't explain why I didn't leave. Probably, because I had nowhere to go. Maybe also because I didn't spend much time at home anyway – the orchestra was often on tour. Or maybe because of Ida, whose sole request was that I didn't leave them. "You and Misha," she said to me once, "can bite each other as much as you want until you lose your minds. But know this, daughter, if you and Gerochka leave you'll be sending me to my grave."

Wise Ida, who had lived a difficult and unusual life, realized that if I left her apartment that would signify the end of my relations with Misha, for whom I (and she was sure of this) meant so much.

I don't know if I would have remained mentally stable in this challenging situation – probably not – if it wasn't for my psychological lightning conductor – the Minister. At that time, he was my pillar of strength.

Naturally, the story with L. number two also ended, and also not without incident. They definitely split up in Moscow, and

L. number two swallowed a bunch of sleeping tablets. Admittedly, this was done in the presence of several of her friends, who managed to save her. For Misha, this "suicide attempt" was the final straw in their affair and he dumped her.

One of my and Misha's friends in common held a birthday party, and he separately invited both of us – at the time, Misha was in Riga. L. number two had by then been out of the picture for some time. He drank heavily that evening, brought me home, and begged me yet again to forget everything and return to him. Again, I refused.

He was now totally single and found this hard to handle. He viewed himself as defeated but couldn't reconcile himself with that fact. A grandmaster said to me once: "When Misha finds himself in a hopeless position, his head tells him this but he doesn't believe that he, Tal, has no chances. He starts to seek a saving combination, convinced that such a combination exists – it's just a matter of locating it. And as a rule he finds it. However, despite all its beauty and numerous sacrifices, the combination turns out to be flawed, and then the defeat becomes for him even more painful and humiliating than if he had been physically dragged face down in the road."

Well, finding himself single and defeated in his private life, Misha himself got caught out in an awful, ghastly, humiliating combination a few years later.

But before I tell you about it, which was a turning point in Misha's life, and in mine to some extent, I want to highlight certain circumstances that preceded that nightmare event.

Friction had appeared in my relations with the Minister. He had remarried. His wife was fully aware of my existence. She would create the most terrible scenes at home and wanted to smash the TV down on his head whenever she saw me performing in some program. My name was subject to the most

unbelievable epithets. I had no need for this, naturally, and
came to the view that we needed to break up, that is, to stop,
as that would be better for both him and me. On the one hand,
he realized that we couldn't continue like that, but, on the
other, due to his huge selfishness, he was unable to let go of me.
He told me that he didn't need anything from me except the
knowledge that I was there and that he could see me. He then
bought me an apartment to which I moved from Gorky Street
(I sold that apartment when I emigrated). Gera's dream came
true – he had always wanted us to live together, just the two of
us. Ida and Robert were quite put out that we left.

Ida realized that with my leaving the chances of my
returning to Misha were practically zero. Nevertheless, Gera
and I continued to spend considerable time in their home and
to treat them as family. Robert and Ida both phoned me several
times a day. Meanwhile, the chief conductor of radio and TV,
Alnis Zakis, was appointed Director of the Riga Entertainment
Orchestra. Soon after meeting him, our relations developed
into something quite different. This was remarkable, as Zakis,
a convinced anti-Semite and Latvian nationalist, fell madly in
love with this one-hundred-percent Jewish girl, abandoned his
family on my account and moved in with us, to my son's great
resentment. Actually, I could only guess about this resentment –
Gera, like Misha, was always incredibly tactful.

My relations with Misha became more settled, although he
continued to phone me from all corners of the Earth. He insisted
I introduce him to Alnis. He said that he didn't have the right to
hand over such a "treasure" as me to the first person I met. Once
at our place, he waited until Alnis went into the kitchen, to say:
"My darling, if you were a chess player and I were your coach,
I would point out that you have selected the wrong plan." Alnis
returned right then, and Misha suddenly sang out: "I have told

you not all the words," as though nothing had happened. They then sang the rest of the song as a duet.

Misha was such a unique person! I was living with Alnis; at the time he was effectively a common-law husband; and Misha understood that perfectly well. And yet, while he treated Alnis with respect, he continued to consider me his only woman and the most important woman in the world – his Saska. Alnis and I left for a tour of East Germany, and Misha came to the station to see me off. Alnis's hands were occupied with the bags and suitcases, so I carried his violin. Misha approached me, took the violin and carried it! People around winked at each other – everybody knew everything, yet for Misha this was totally natural: it was heavy or difficult for Saska to carry, so he had to help her. And who cared whose violin it was – Alnis Zakis's or David Oistrakh's.

Fast forwarding, I want to say that Misha then took an interest in every guy with whom I had a relationship. He wanted to know everything possible about the person. He sort of gave me his blessing. Boris Spassky once said to me: "Sally, I believe that Misha is just causing you pain." But no, he wasn't trying to cause me pain – he wanted to be by my side. And of all my men, it was only the Minister whom he couldn't stand, and that was because he saw a real rival in him. Alnis took quite a liking to Misha, saw what a remarkable person he was, and would say of him: "Tal isn't a Jew. Tal is a chess genius."

Even after I moved out, Ida never gave up the notion that I would return, and whenever we spoke she would raise the matter of my relations with Misha: "Misha is lonely," "Misha is depressed," "Misha is ill," "Misha is in hospital again."

However, I was worried about Misha, too, as the nearest and dearest person to me. I knew that he was suffering with his illnesses that remained recognized by nobody. I did everything I could for him. Not out of duty, but as my heart instructed. Even under extreme pressure I couldn't have acted differently. Obviously, thoughts about our possible reconciliation and restarting with him did occur to me, but each time that happened images of L. number one and L. number two would appear before my eyes with renewed impulse. I knew that should I give in to Ida's and Misha's exhortations yet another L. would appear before too long. Or an F.. I couldn't accept that, ever. Maybe that was my eternal misfortune, I don't know.

So this was the background to summer 1970, when Ida made friends at the Riga seaside with an intelligent, elderly Georgian lady who turned out to be a former princess. By the way, Ida told me that when she mentioned to Misha that she had met a former princess Misha immediately objected: "Murochka! A princess cannot be 'former' any more than a St. Bernard can be 'former'. It's a noble breed, Murochka, not a job description."

In a nutshell, Ida becomes acquainted with this very old princess, they get chatting, and the princess tells Ida about her granddaughter – a charming young lady whose parents tragically split up and whom she essentially brought up herself. The girl, according to the princess, is fantastically talented, refined, has wonderful manners, writes beautiful poetry, and what is more – has a dash of Jewish blood through her great-grandmother. Basically, "an angel". However, she has suffered a terrible woe: she has been dating the champion of Georgia (either at boxing or wrestling), loves this man, but he categorically refuses to marry her. That's the story that the Georgian princess tells Ida about this "mermaid". On top of all that, the princess produces a photo: she's a true beauty, like a classical statue, with huge blue innocent eyes. Ida tells me this straight away: Ida never hid anything from me, not even the tiniest of details. But this time, I catch her really focusing on these details: intelligent, unhappy, talented, good manners, as lonely as Misha. I heard her out but said nothing – it wasn't the most captivating of stories.

Meanwhile, Misha continued to suffer awful pains emanating from his kidneys with "an unclear etiology", as the doctors said. Well, it just so happens that he gets sent at this point to Tbilisi, the Georgian capital, to a famous urologist surgeon. The surgeon insists on an operation and Misha is given a place in the best hospital in Georgia. Right then, Ida phones the Georgian princess and they devise an elaborate plan to set up this "mermaid" with Misha. It was like Ida had drunk a potion of vitality! She was in a super mood – maybe, at long last, Misha would find happiness, maybe they would fall in love, even marry. All the more so, as Misha was adored in Georgia, they treated him like a God. Ida even said that for the sake of Misha's happiness and wellbeing the entire family could uproot and move to Georgia, where Yasha would find a job.

They met. Ida told me that Misha was enchanted by the girl, that she liked him too, that she would visit him in the hospital and write poems about him. Ida is happy – thank God, a pure and innocent creature has appeared, not a random woman, isn't an alcoholic, isn't greedy and isn't dreaming of finding a rich and famous husband and squeezing him like a lemon. Ida reads me over the phone the girl's poems about Misha, in which she writes that she has never in her life met a man with such charm, such humor, such intelligence and such manners. Basically, knowing Ida, knowing Misha, knowing Robert, I realize that they have collectively imagined some huge colorful pipe dream called love. And so one day, Robert phones me and says: "Dear Sally – we need to meet. We need to have a serious conversation." I agree, invite him over, and think to myself: "I expect I have to do something for Misha again."

"I don't even know how to explain this, Sallynka," Robert began. "You know that Misha now has a girlfriend whom he loves and who really loves him. Maybe we will all move to Georgia soon. Please grant Misha a divorce. Know that you will always remain our darling Sallynka, and Gerochka will always remain our grandson."

"Robert, I agree. What do we need to do?"

"Misha is in hospital currently. So you have to do it all yourself. I've agreed matters with the magistrate, she'll process it quickly and without making a commotion."

The next day, I showed up at court. There was nobody in the little room apart from the magistrate. I told her: "I want to divorce Mikhail Tal." Robert really had smoothed things. She asked me just one question: "Which surname do you want to bear, Tal or Landau?" – "Landau."

I left the court a divorced woman. I walked out to head for home and thought: "Misha and I married in an instant and without a commotion. And we've divorced in an instant and without a commotion. And that's it." I started to feel down.

I arrived at a square opposite the opera house, sat down on a bench and couldn't move for a couple of hours.

Sometime later, I learnt that Georgian TV had shown a plush and pompous wedding. In the best Georgian style: Georgia was giving the hand of its beautiful daughter in marriage to a huge genius, the great Mikhail Tal. Apparently, a zealous Georgian journalist had dug deep into Tal's family tree and found some Georgian roots.

The bride was dressed up beautifully, of course. Misha in a dinner suit. Basically, all the expected trimmings. They showed the guests singing songs, they showed the couple signing at the registry office. Apparently, even Vasil Mzhavanadze (I think he was the First Secretary of the Georgian Communist Party

Central Committee at the time) blessed the young couple. I thought back to our own "wedding" and I felt a little offended as a woman. Then I began to imagine the entire process, with singing and dancing, Misha in a dinner suit doing his utmost to look serene, and I found the picture amusing: this just wasn't Misha.

While a student, Misha wrote his undergraduate dissertation on Ilf and Petrov's book *The Twelve Chairs*. He knew most of their works just about by heart and could recite entire chapters. And now here he was, the hero of a tragicomedy that would have embellished any of Ilf and Petrov's works.

About a month after the ceremony, Ida called me in total bewilderment: "If you don't get over here right now I don't know what will happen to me!" I get into my car (I was a huge rarity in those days – a Soviet woman who could drive and owned her own car), show up at the apartment and learn from Ida the following. The young couple arrive in Moscow and check into a hotel. Everything's great and wonderful. But a few days later, the young bride ups and disappears. Leaves as though to deal with some matter and doesn't return by nightfall. Misha's panicking. Goes out looking for her, drags the police out to help. The bride then returns a full day later and tells him that her boyfriend from Tbilisi, whom she has loved passionately her entire life, has shown up, that he swears that he loves only her and wants to take her away and marry her, and wants a child with her, and that if he can't have her then he'll kill himself. Basically, she tells Misha that she's returning to her sweetheart, says sorry that things have turned out that way, and asks him not to be angry at her. A nervous laughter takes hold of me, but Ida is weeping – this is a true tragedy for her. She is in no doubt that all of this was contrived in advance: knowing the psychology of Georgian men, the young Georgian girl married Tal and got the wedding to be shown on TV throughout the country; her boyfriend would feel shamed and vow to win back his beloved not only from Tal but from the Devil himself, that it's now a matter of principle.

So there's Ida swearing damnation at this cunning lass for using Misha in order to win back her boxing or wrestling champion. She tells me that Misha phoned her, told her everything, that he's in shock and can't for the life of him understand how it could have happened.

As far as I know, Misha never again discussed the "Georgian affair" with anybody. This was a massive blow, from which he needed a very long time to recover. I can only guess how painful it was. You see, Misha was innocent to the point of naivety and incredibly self-confident. He had been caught in a Talesque combination of his own, he hadn't foreseen any sacrifices, he already heard the fanfare of victory and suddenly, one move before the long-awaited triumph, he was being told: "Wake up, Maestro, you've been checkmated!"

"My daughter," Ida said to me, "she has simply destroyed him! I don't know how he'll get over this story, I can't even think how to help him... He said that he has become even more convinced that there is no woman in the world more pure and loyal than his Saska. What do you think about that?"

I took this as another offer to go back to old times. I knew that Misha would be overjoyed to live with me again. But I was tired and incapable of any more self-sacrificing exertions. Above all, I realized then more than ever that Misha would always remain "the genius Tal", and that any woman who hooked up with him would be recognized by everybody at "the wife of the genius Tal". Well, with my personality, I couldn't be so yielding, prepared to put up with everything in order to be the wife of a genius, no matter what I thought of Misha, no matter how much I loved him.

Misha again found himself in a vacuum. It's hard, probably impossible to imagine the loneliness that the romantic and deep thinker Tal felt.

Soon after, he met Gelya at the Riga Chess Club. She became his wife and remained so until Misha's death. She was loyal, long-suffering, loving, and the mother of his daughter, Zhannochka.

I don't know what would have happened to him, what level of chess he would have played, how long he would have survived even, if it wasn't for Gelya. Gelya, being much younger than Misha, devoted herself entirely to the genius Tal, understood and discerned all of Misha's subtleties and nuances, and kept up with his crazy rhythm. I will venture to say this: Misha valued in Gelya everything that he wanted to receive from me.

At first, I was indifferent to Gelya as Misha's wife and I treated her as another victim of his "vortex". But after Zhanna was born, I suddenly found myself feeling something akin to jealousy. Not as a woman, but more as the mother of his son. I always felt that Misha as a father didn't devote enough attention to Gera. And after Zhannochka's birth Gera would lose even that tiny amount. However, I was mistaken. The more Gera grew, the greater Misha's love for him became. Misha seemed surprised, discovering that his Goosevich had grown into an adult with whom he could hold an adult conversation and to whom he could even entrust his male secrets, being sure that Gera wouldn't share them with anybody. Suddenly, he noticed that his Goosevich had become a student at the medical institute, which accepted him at 15(!)[19]. He often returned to the subject:

---

[19] The normal age for starting a higher education degree in the Soviet Union was 17

"Goose when he was little refuted the dubious axiom that intelligence isn't passed on from parents to children." Misha at first also treated the baby Zhanna with tenderness and delight, like a favorite toy.

Misha, especially after the birth of his daughter, started to invite me over with increasing persistence. He was anxious to introduce me to Gelya. He kept telling me what an amazing woman she was, and that he was certain she and I would become friends. So I eventually agreed to go round and meet her. I won't pretend anything – at first I was reserved in my interactions with her, exaggeratedly polite, and as a woman I noted for myself: "She doesn't do this right or that right, I would do everything quite differently." But I adored Zhannochka from the beginning, not only like a charming infant. I caught myself immediately thinking of her as Gera's sister, as Misha's daughter, as though she were my daughter. Misha was desperate for Gelya and I to treat each other warmly, as close relations. It's as though he wanted to prove at the same time: isn't Gelya wonderful, and isn't my Saska wonderful!

After Misha's funeral we returned to the apartment on Gorky Street and Gelya and I just sat in silence. I was thinking that we had both lost *our* Misha, that he was gone for her and for me.

In the early 1970s, a nightclub opened in Riga with what at the time were genuine European standards. Aino Balina and many other famous performers would sing there. There was a rich and varied program, and I was invited to work there. They promised me significantly higher pay than the salary I earned from the Riga Entertainment Orchestra, and so I agreed – we were short of money at the time, and I continued to refuse to become a "kept woman".

You couldn't just walk into the nightclub where I sang. You had to book in advance, and the bar would not accept reservations from just anybody. It was always cordoned off by the police. VIPs often held sumptuous receptions here. Well, I made no effort to befriend the ministers who hung out there. A mistake, as it turned out. They could have come in useful – Jews were beginning to leave Latvia...

Grigory Efimovich, the administrator of the Riga Youth Theater, left for Israel in 1967 with his family. That evening, when half of Riga came to see him off, he told me: "Sally, what's keeping you here? Leave. We'll send you an invitation. Leave for your son's sake. It's pointless staying here." His words took root in me and soon I began to think about leaving the Soviet Union. I didn't have much of a clue what I would do abroad without having any real professional qualifications, but I vacuously believed that I would get by. All the more so as there were previous examples. The popular singer Larisa Mondrus had left with her husband Egils Svarcs, my friend Vida Vaitkute, with whom I had worked in the orchestra in Lithuania, left with her husband. And after that, my very best friend, Inna Mandelstam, also left. So did many others. I too got infected by the emigration epidemic.

So I really began to think seriously about it. There was no doubt in my mind that Gerochka would leave with me. I once broached the subject with Misha. At first, he didn't think I was serious, laughing it off with: "Do you want to emigrate with the threat of moving back?" This was a sort of joke familiar to his chess crowd. If his opponent in a friendly game made a bad move, Misha often reacted with a comment along the lines of "You're moving queen a5 with the threat of moving back?"

Once I made him understand that my intentions were serious, he replied quite firmly: "Do what you want, but I'm not letting Goose leave!" I don't know what the laws are now, but in those days of the Soviet Union a child could only leave with his mother subject to his father's permission, and vice versa. I returned to this subject several times after that, but Misha consistently replied "No."

I appealed to the party Central Committee. They told me that once my child reached a majority age, 18, he could decide himself whether or not to emigrate with me. So I had to wait. However, it then transpired, once Gera reached 18, that his emigration still required Misha's permission (as mentioned in Chapter 2). And Misha's view was unchanged. Anyway, at that point Gera didn't want to emigrate. He was already in his third year at university and had a girlfriend, Nadia, whom he loved and whom he later married. He couldn't give up his studies or leave his beloved girl there.

Nevertheless, the idea of leaving became a fixation for me, and I decided I would hence leave on my own, at the very least at first. My idea was to leave Gera our apartment and some money so that he would join me in emigration after he graduated. However, a good-looking but greying officer who interviewed me in the OVIR[20] told me crisply that they would not let me leave on my own (again, as Gera mentioned). When Gera heard this, he decided to leave with me. He then went to see his father.

Misha told him: "You're an adult. Make your own decision." At the same time, he didn't want to sign permission for Gera to leave. I think it was because he didn't want any trouble with the authorities. He wasn't afraid for his personal safety, but I'm sure he was afraid that it would have harmed his chess career, without which he couldn't imagine his life.

---

[20] Office of Visas and Registrations – a Soviet government agency whose responsibilities included all matters of visas and residence

Ultimately, they could have again banned him from travelling, all the more so as by then the authorities had found younger and more compliant favorites among chess players. Misha was never a party member. After he became world champion the party Central Committee leadership "gently" suggested that he join, but Misha politely refused, citing his fragile health and busy chess schedule. So you can see he was never afraid personally to take a stance.

Ida solved that problem, saying that the document requiring Misha's signature should be delivered to the apartment at a time when he was absent and that Gelya would forge Misha's signature without his knowledge. And that's what happened: the letter arrived, Misha wasn't in Riga, Gelya signed it surreptitiously and Gera and I received permission to leave. Misha wasn't in Riga when we left either, so we never said our goodbyes.

Ida was critically ill by the time we left. She was in hospital and would die soon after. By then, she mostly didn't recognize people. Gera and I went to see her on the eve of our journey. Robert said: "Saska, don't go into her room. Don't cause yourself any grief. She won't recognize you, anyway." "Well, I'll at least go and kiss her," I replied. "We are flying off tomorrow." I went into her room and took her by the hand. Suddenly, she opened her eyes, looked at me with absolute clarity, and said: "My daughter... see how everything is just fine? I told you, everything would be fine, and you didn't believe me. You and Gerochka are leaving, and everything will be fine there. Only, don't leave Misha on his own."

And she closed her eyes.

The next day, we flew off to Moscow, and from there we flew to Vienna. It was 1 July 1979.

We had left the Soviet Union on an Israeli visa, but I had no plans to go to Israel. Once in Vienna, those emigrating would attempt to sort out their future. My friend, who by then had set up home in Dusseldorf, told us to go to Germany, that she would fill in all the necessary documents. But I hesitated. Those who made it to Vienna but didn't go on to Israel were normally sent to Italy, and that's what happened to us. Once in Italy, I received a letter from Inna Mandelstam. She was now living in Canada, and wrote that she had filled in all the necessary documents for us to move there. However, Gera put his foot down: "Mum, I want to remain in Europe. Dad often travels to Europe and I want to see him." Sometime later, we ended up in Berlin.

Although times were tough at first as immigrants in Vienna and Italy, positive emotions prevailed. I was struck by Vienna's beauty, while Italy left me feeling exhilarated – even today, the name "Italy" leaves me feeling joyful. We were driven in a car from Italy to Munich. I can't say that I felt entirely free. That came much later. I simply thought to myself during the journey: "So there you are, Sally, you're abroad again." And I couldn't help recalling that already distant and sweet time when I first travelled abroad, as Mikhail Tal's wife. Heavens, I was so happy then!

It was in 1962, at the candidates tournament on Curacao. The tournament lasted two months, and there was a two-week break in the middle when it was decided that the players' wives could join them at this holiday resort. Of course, we had to pay ourselves, but we were still grateful for the invitation. In those days, travelling abroad, and especially to capitalist countries, was just a pipe-dream for the vast majority of Soviet citizens. And suddenly here was a chance! An island with such a romantic name! Curacao! Obviously, we didn't have the money for the trip. But one wall in the Tal apartment sported a huge painting by some famous Latvian artist, and Robert decided to sell it. This money paid for my voyage.

Before we went, the wives (Geller's, Petrosian's, Korchnoi's and Keres's wives and me) were called into the party Central Committee and given a pep-talk – by a functionary who when he finished had great trouble locating Curacao on the huge map on his wall. Above all, we were told to avoid mixing with the local men.

We flew to Amsterdam via a Dutch airline. Amsterdam wowed me with its amazing cleanliness and calm, pleasant inhabitants. It was like I had reached Heaven. I had the impression that people there never died. At the time, I couldn't have imagined that Amsterdam would many years later become quite an ordinary city for me that I could drive to in my own car in an hour-and-a-half or so. But then, during my first trip abroad, I had to pinch myself to believe that I was in Amsterdam(!) – a city which, like all foreign cities, had been nothing but a geographical point on a map up until then.

Actually, we had an adventure on the way. We flew from Amsterdam to somewhere else, I forget now, and from there to Caracas. We were then meant to fly from Caracas to Curacao. However, when the plane started up a wing caught fire! As a result, we had to spend two nights in the airplane until it was fixed. Our passports were taken from us so we couldn't go anywhere, whereas some local people on the flight were put up in a hotel.

It was very sunny in Amsterdam. In fact, that entire trip remained in my memory as a period of endless sunlight, in both the literal and indirect senses. We were met by a tall, distinguished-looking man with aristocratic mannerisms. He turned out to be ex-world champion Max Euwe. He talked with us and asked us some questions, all in German. However, I had only studied English in school and couldn't understand a word of what he was saying. I simply replied "yes" or "no". Often guessing wrongly... They organized two sightseeing tours for us – to the diamond factory, which left all the GMs' wives feeling quite depressed, and then on a little ferry along the canals. I was won over by this amazing country, and when I reached Curacao I remember telling Misha that I would love to live in Holland. We stayed there until the end of the tournament, and when we left Curacao and flew back via Amsterdam we were again met by Euwe. Misha and the other players stayed for a while in Europe under the watchful eye of the KGB and the delegation head Gorshkov, making money from simuls (half of which they had to surrender to the state). In that month and a half in Curacao I'd managed to pick up a little more of what I assumed to be German, and Euwe told Misha: "When your wife was last here she could only say 'yes' and 'no', and only in English. Yet it turns out she speaks excellent German!" I was immensely proud of that praise, to which Misha responded: "I don't understand how Dr. Euwe managed to read the entire works of Sholem Aleichem in Yiddish in just two months." Well, it turned out that I was talking to Euwe in Yiddish words that I'd picked up, which had much in common with German...

...We read the newspaper headlines about Tal throughout the world: "Pirate of the chess board", "Lover of adventure", "Chess rocket", "Wizard from Riga", "Founder of the neo-psychological school", "Vortex from the Soviet Union", "Morphy of our days". Well, let's analyze these descriptions in a little more detail.

"Pirate of the chess board". This is incorrect. Tal isn't a pirate, he's a brave chess player, dangerous to play against, takes big risks, plays unsound sacrifices...

"Lover of adventure". This epithet is somewhat softer, it sounds nicer: a romantic in chess. Many of Tal's games are imbued with this spirit...

"Wizard from Riga". I think this means a manner of playing that is difficult to understand and which with pedantic precision reaches the target.

"Chess rocket". This underlines Tal's incredible tempo, unusual energy and his decisiveness...

"Morphy of our days". This description refers to Tal's sharpness and brilliance at the board, proved by many of his games...

"Founder of the neo-psychological school". Tal has claimed on more than one occasion that he chooses not the strongest move but the one that places his opponent in a more difficult situation...

What a huge range of names, and so many traits! Clearly, Tal has something of every previous world champion in him. Brilliance from Morphy, magic from Steinitz, a psychological approach from Lasker, an incredible tempo from Alekhine, energy from Botvinnik. The only thing he lacks is Smyslov's calm judgement...

Dr. Max Euwe , ex-world champion, *Ogoniok,* 1960

Of all the seven other tournament players, it was the young Fischer who struck me the most. This well-built and self-confident early developer, living in a world of his own, often made a bizarre impression (away from the chess board, obviously). He resembled a huge child whose parents had delivered the entire world to his feet, and said: "Bobby, it's all yours!" And whenever life rubbed his face in the dirt he would be genuinely shocked and get really wound up, unable to understand how he, the great Bobby, could be treated so badly. He lived entirely for chess and had a firm grip on his chess life. However, he was totally unadjusted to everyday society. Well, Fischer had to be accepted for what he was, without imposing any external standards on him. You had to get used to him, and then you would discover a kind and warm human being. We ended up getting on very well with each other.

Misha had once taken my photo off the wall of a theater foyer and pocketed it. Since then, he insisted on taking that photo with him permanently. Like a lucky charm. "Your photo brings me luck," he told me. One day, when Misha was flying off to Sochi, we forgot in the rush to put that photo in his luggage. And guess what? In Sochi, Misha was caught in a car accident. Fortunately, it was nothing serious. But afterwards he would say that had my photo been with him the accident wouldn't have happened.

Generally speaking, Misha believed in omens. After I emigrated, I once came to visit him in Brussels during a tournament. I was shocked at his awful suit, crumpled and dirty shirt, and shoes with worn out heels. It wasn't that he didn't have any money. Of course he had money. But he just didn't seem to care about himself. And I told him: "Misha! If you're going to go around looking like that I won't come and visit you again! It's embarrassing!" So Ratko Knezevic and I went out and bought him a new suit, shirt, tie and shoes, and we just about had to use force to get him to wear them. That day, he lost his game and was furious. "This is all down to your masquerade!" he complained. "Mishanka!" I replied, "don't tell me you never lost a game in your old shirt!" "In my old shirt I lose because it's my fault," he retorted, "but in this peasant outfit I lose because it's your fault... See the difference?"

So to return to Fischer – when Misha showed him that same photo, Bobby spent a considerable amount of time admiring it, and then simply expropriated it from Misha. He as though borrowed it but never gave it back. If Fischer came across us on the beach he would come and sit with us, unceremoniously shoving Misha away with his elbow and engaging me in long conversations. He spoke in broken Russian. Given that the most important chess literature was published at the time in the USSR he had learnt some of the language. Bobby had only gained a limited schooling, and when I asked him why he'd never graduated from school, he replied: "Because school got in the way of my chess." He was an amusing guy. A local millionaire invited us to a little restaurant on the other side of the island. Fischer sat in the car next to me and turned the radio on. He found a channel where some guy was singing and suddenly began to sing loudly alongside him. He was tone-deaf! A truly awful voice! And then he said to me in total seriousness: "If I weren't a great chess player I would have become a great singer."

...One day, a very young Fischer showed up at the excellent baritone Smyslov's hotel room during a rest period and started to hum something. Vasily Vasilevich, who was by nature a very gentle person, told him: "Bobby! You are really talented!" These words put wind in the American grandmaster's sails. Two years later, there was Fischer telling everybody what a great singer he was. During the tournament in Bled we played a little trick on him. One evening, we all gathered in a bar where an orchestra was playing, accompanying a singer. Somebody had a word with the compere and we heard him announce: "Ladies and gentlemen! We are now going to be treated to a performance by the amazing American chess player and singer Robert James Fischer!" Fischer got all shy but nevertheless took the microphone. He sang, let's say, idiosyncratically. The audience nevertheless gave him a huge ovation. He then headed back to his seat, accepting the congratulations, and stopped by Paul Keres's table. Keres told him: "You should give up chess and switch to singing." Whereupon Fischer replied: "Yes, I know, but I'm too good at chess."

Mikhail Tal, extract from an interview in *64*, 1979

Misha was very nice to Bobby and treated him humorously. Apparently, he once beat Fischer and then decided to goof around with: "Bobby! Cuckoo!" Fischer burst into tears like an infant. But Misha was the first person to say that Fischer was a real genius and a future world champion.

Actually, Misha had great relations with almost every chess player. He was especially close to Petrosian, Karpov and Geller. He treated Korchnoi respectfully, tactfully, which you couldn't have said about me – I wasn't fond of the man at all.

Paul Keres also stood out among the humdrum crowd. Handsome, respectable looking, polite and genuinely sporty. He was a fantastic swimmer, and every morning at eight a.m. you would find him in the pool. During a rest day, when we were getting ready to descend to breakfast, Misha told me: "Go downstairs, take a swim with Keres, go for breakfast and I'll arrive shortly."

Breakfast was over. We were all sunbathing by the pool, but Misha and Fischer hadn't shown up. Fischer always ignored the swimming pool anyway – he would spend his entire time studying chess in his room. An hour passed, then another, then another... Still no Misha. I checked our room several times, but he wasn't there. The head of our delegation, Yuri Averbakh, as well as the "art expert in civilian clothes", started to worry. They even sent people over to French quarter. Misha wasn't there either and we still had no news. Lunch came and went and I got very worried. In fact, everybody got worried. I started to fear that something serious had happened – Misha was always prone to illness, after all. Anything could have happened. Nightfall approached. Nobody could go to bed – they all hung around the large hotel lobby on the second floor, everybody proffering their own version of events.

And then suddenly, at midnight, the door of the press center opened. The center was closed on rest days and its door was normally locked. Two completely bedraggled men emerged with mad eyes – Misha and Bobby. Misha walked past me, clearly not registering that I was there, and headed for our bedroom. It transpired that, early that morning, Fischer had persuaded Tal to lock themselves in the press center and play blitz, the idea being that I wouldn't nag Misha to come and sit by the pool or drag him into town. And so they played non-stop from eight-thirty in the morning until midnight. I don't know how many games they played, but I understood that Misha won.

Not even the "art expert" accompanying us could ruin that golden trip. He was an odd-looking chap who intervened in everything: he hung about with us by the pool, wandered around the market and shops with us, and sat in the press center during the games asking our and the foreign coaches ridiculous questions about the moves played by the grandmasters.

Unfortunately, Misha was unable to finish the tournament. Once again, he was held hostage by awful kidney pains and was sent to hospital in the French quarter, where they suggested he stay and undergo a detailed examination. However, he categorically refused, and discharged himself as soon as he felt a little better. The chief doctor at the hospital, a very nice man, stepped back from medical recommendations and told him as he was leaving: "It's awful in your country. They arrest you and send you to Siberia. Leave your wife here at the very least. She's so young, so beautiful... I like her." Misha smiled and answered: "You like her here, but I will love her in Siberia if I have to."

Oh, it was an unforgettable time! I befriended Rona and Tigran Petrosian on Curacao. Tigran was an incredible guy. He loved Misha and always envied his "warrior-like health". I remember the Petrosians inviting me over in Moscow while I was working for Rosner. They were wonderful hosts. Naturally, we discussed Misha, whose affair with L. was in full swing by then. Rona asked me: "Sally, tell us truthfully, are you angry with Misha? Do you want him to suffer?" "Heaven forbid!" I replied.

"I just want him to be happy!" "Then you still love him," Rona concluded. Tigran accompanied me to the taxi. I looked at him and suddenly suggested: "We'd better kiss. What if we never see each other again." "We will see each other again!" Tigran replied. "Why on Earth not?"

Well, I never saw him again...

40 years later, the island of Curacao decided to remind the chess world, and indeed the wider world, of its existence. The Internet, radio, TV and newspapers were suddenly awash with reports that in honor of that great tournament the island would host a kind of continuation. Alas, only two of the eight participants showed up – Pal Benko and Viktor Korchnoi. Fischer had by then left the chess scene, while the others had completed their time on Earth. Yuri Averbakh, who had been Tal's second in 1962, also went. Invited by the organizers, he visited the very same restaurant where he had eaten every day forty years earlier – and received a wonderful surprise: the orchestra was playing one of the travel songs of the famous Soviet bard Yuri Vizbor about snow swirling above a tent. And this on a tropical island which had never experienced a single snow drop in its entire existence!

Averbakh, with his innate inquisitiveness, carried out a quick survey among the musicians. Some had inherited their instruments – and, indeed, their places in the orchestra – from their fathers who played in that very same restaurant in 1962. Well, among the women who had come to stay with their husbands competing in the candidates tournament, there had been a fiery red-headed singer who was invited up on stage those forty years before. She had sung to the players, and the musicians had gradually picked up the tune, so that her song was soon heard in all its splendor throughout the restaurant. Ever since 1962, both the islands' residents and guests listen to that same song, and learn about Russian snow.

Surely I don't have to tell you who that red-headed beauty was...

Yakov Damsky, added to the 2006 (3rd) Russian edition of this book

Salo Flohr, with whom I was great friends, once showed me around the Moscow chess club, and told me, pointing at the photos of world champions on the wall: "Sallynka, look at them. They are all the most normal, mad people." Well, I'm ever thankful that I lived my life among such "normal, mad people" as Misha, Tigran, Bobby, and Tolya Karpov. (Garry Kasparov is also a genius, but not mad – that's my opinion, anyway.)

So those sweet memories were playing inside my half sleeping head as Gerochka and I travelled in the car from Italy to Munich, to a completely unknown future...

We then moved from Munich to Berlin. Our most difficult years in emigration were those that we spent in Berlin. I have noticed a certain law. People who left the Soviet Union and more or less arranged a decent new life for themselves eagerly and sincerely advised their friends and relatives who had stayed behind to do the same. Yes, at first it would be difficult, but everything would sort itself out in the end. Of course it would! Anything else would be unthinkable! Soviet emigres will tell you this rather inelegant axiom: "Everybody needs to eat their own portion of shit." Therefore, when you first arrive and begin to eat shit, everybody considers this activity to be absolutely standard, they all sympathize with you, although none of them cares to share your meal.

I don't wish anybody to put up with what I had to endure in those years. No job, you don't know the language. You need money to pick up German, but you don't have any because you don't have a job. You don't have a job because you don't know the language. We found ourselves in a vicious circle where we felt second-class citizens needed by nobody. We immediately became foreigners, in the European sense of the word. Europeans don't have the servile attitude to foreigners characteristic of Soviet people. The French and, in particular, the Germans consider themselves to be superior, and everybody else, especially immigrants, to be inferior. You don't see this trait exhibited explicitly, but you sense it with your skin. You sense it even more when you have no money.

Our hopes that Gera would be able to continue his education in a German university went up in smoke. Gera stubbornly refused to write in his documents that his father, grandmother and entire family on his father's side were genetic "inheritors of German culture". As a result, he was granted a residence permit for aliens – for an *auslander*. Moreover, with incredible competition for places at the medical university (500 candidates per place) his chances were obviously zero. We were allocated monthly welfare totalling 350 DM. I can't imagine what would have happened to us. But I've been lucky all my life. Lucky enough to come across good, decent, kind people.

First, we were helped finding a wonderful apartment that welfare paid for. Then, we were introduced to a Russian guy who had lived in Leningrad prior to emigration. He was called Boris, and had a truly "revolutionary" surname – Bukharin. He was young, practical, a born businessman. He specialized in icons. Quite the smooth operator. He made big money, but was useless at saving it. He spent it on women, for whom he had a particular weakness, and parted with thousands in restaurants and casinos. If it wasn't for these passions, I think that he would have been one of the richest immigrants around. He started to tag along with us, especially with me. I think he hit on me. He took Gera and me to Italy, bought us clothes and shoes, fed us...

Bought us presents, and never showed up without a bouquet of flowers.

After Gera returned to the Soviet Union, Boris even asked me to marry him, but I couldn't imagine life with such a high roller and womanizer. And I turned him down. He gradually distanced himself from me, but I'm endlessly grateful to him for his support in those two difficult years.

Misha came to Holland for a tournament in Tilburg and stopped over in Amsterdam. He phoned and said that he was waiting for us there. It was our first encounter since we emigrated. I never expected us to meet up in Europe more frequently than in our last years in the Soviet Union, but we did.

That first meeting was preceded by a number of phone calls. Gera phoned his father in the USSR frequently and Misha called us from there just as often. It was late 1980, more than four years prior to the end of the period of stagnation and the start of Perestroika. Soviet people who had emigrated to the West were viewed by both the country's government and the man in the street as traitors to the motherland. Not only close, but also distant relatives of emigrants were destined to face big problems. The authorities kept watch over them and they risked losing their jobs. Misha maintained phone contact with us, aware that the calls were bugged. When we arrived in Amsterdam, I asked him: "Do you realize you can get into trouble?" He replied: "Saska, I will do what I want. I'll calculate the sidelines later." I told Misha everything: that we were living on welfare, that it was practically impossible for Gera to gain a study place, that I didn't have a job, that I'd only begun to study German at the Goethe Institute, that the suburbs of Berlin were disgusting, that narcotics were sold in the subway there, and that because of all that I was dreadfully worried about Gera's future.

I realized that Gera was made of pretty obstinate fibers. I remember well saying to Ida when he won a place at medical institute in Latvia that I was afraid his medical training would turn him cynical and heartless. She replied: "Don't you worry about Gerochka. His genes are too good. That's out of the question!"

Nevertheless, I was afraid. I asked Misha: "What do you think, perhaps Gera should return to the Soviet Union and complete his degree there?" I remember his instant reaction: "You're crazy!" Then they sent me to go for a walk and remained chatting, just the two of them. Misha told Gera that first he would try to arrange a visitor's visa. He realized that he was going to carry a big responsibility on his shoulders. Gera received a visitor's visa to the Soviet Union soon after Misha had left. He went there and returned, in a great mood. "Mum, it's looking like I'm going to return there." "How come?" "Dad said that he will arrange everything," Gera replied.

And "Dad arranged everything." One can only guess what it cost Misha to get his son to be allowed to resume his studies in Latvia. I think that there were only two people at that time in the Soviet Union who were allowed to fully return – Gera Tal and Stalin's daughter Svetlana Alliluyeva.

After Gera left Germany completely, in March 1981, he told me the following: "Mum, I will definitely return. I just beg you, be patient." Well, I couldn't restrain myself and burst into tears. I told him that he wouldn't return to me, that I didn't believe a country that placed its leader in a mausoleum one day and threw him out of it the next, that I was scared he would be called up to fight in Afghanistan, that I was losing him forever, that I had nobody but him. But Gera left, and it was another six years before I saw him again.

After Gera returned to Latvia, I fell into a depression, exacerbated by my awful migraines. I even thought about ending my time on Earth... Vida Vaitkute did her best to drag me out of this state. She invited me over and introduced me to her friends. This eased the pain somewhat but certainly didn't cure it. Then in April, I suddenly got a phone call from Malaga: "I have told you not all the words!" Misha was beseeching me to come and see him in Malaga for several days where he was playing in a tournament. He said he would organize my ticket, that my trip wouldn't cost me anything, and that he desperately wanted to see me. I agreed in an instant. I didn't want to think about anything. His voice had such warm and familiar intonations that for a minute I thought I had gone back twenty years in time. I thought: "How fortunate that Misha phoned right now! It's as though he sensed something."

I immediately felt a burning desire to meet up with Misha. I was missing him. The next day, I received a ticket, money from Misha and a note that the tournament would be held in Costa del Sol. On the plane, I got acquainted with a charming German couple flying to Malaga for their holidays. They took me under their wings, which was a good thing, as otherwise I would have been unlikely to resolve the situation I found myself in when we arrived.

Well, I didn't know the language at all, and had no idea how to get to Costa del Sol, which I had assumed to be the name of another town. They explained that their villa was located in Costa del Sol and so they looked after me. The problem was that when we got to their town, which I took for "Costa del Sol", nobody had a clue what chess tournament I was on about. So I spent two days staying at the German couple's beautiful villa. We spent those two days wandering around their town trying to find out at least a hint of information about the chess tournament. We would say the names "Karpov", "Kasparov", "Tal" – and the people would stare back blankly. Finally, the German guy came up with the idea of drawing chess pieces on a sheet of paper. Whereupon the waiter in some cafe suddenly got excited, saying in his broken English: "Ah! Chess! Chess!.. Malaga! Malaga! Not Costa del Sol! Malaga!" So we figured out that the tournament was actually taking place in Malaga after all, and the next day this kind couple drove me back there. We soon came across a huge knight and a poster advertising the tourney. We found the local police station, where they told us in which hotel the grandmasters were staying, and we showed up at the right place ten minutes later.

A nasty surprise awaited me: Tal wasn't in the hotel. He had been hospitalized. He had felt heart trouble and they sent him to Madrid. But nobody knew to which hospital, and even if they had known, there was nothing more for me to do than to wait. I didn't have any spare money. I didn't know how to travel to Madrid, or how to find him once I got there.

I got extremely anxious, and that is why, when Misha returned several days later from Madrid – suddenly, as though nothing had happened – I gave him "my" present: another migraine attack. When Misha came into the hotel room he took fright:

"What's wrong with you, Saska?"

"Same as usual, Mishanka... What about you?"

Our dialogue resembled that of two disabled war veterans.

"I'm absolutely fine!" he said.

"You had a problem with your heart?"

"My heart was hurting because it was missing its Saska... Now it's fine! You see, the flight was delayed in Leningrad. Apart from the GMs, the aircraft was meant to deliver some paintings from the Hermitage to Italy. I just felt exhausted... But I need to get you up on your feet urgently!"

Of course, this was just bravado — he looked terrible...

"Firstly," said Misha, "I'm taking you into my room."

Several minutes later, the hotel's entire first-aid box was placed at my disposal. Yet had I swallowed the entire lot of pain-killers in a single go I doubt that they would have helped. Misha made a witty joke about this: "Saska, the best way to cure your migraine is with a guillotine." That afternoon, the same kind German couple drove us to the local hospital. There, they couldn't work out what was wrong with me. Misha tried to explain to them, in both German and English, but to no avail. The doctors and nurses stubbornly spoke back only in Spanish. Meanwhile, I was flat out and only semi-conscious, barely opening my eyes.

Misha, almost in tears, tried to convince them to give me a pain-killing injection, but they didn't seem to get it. They just twittered on in their Spanish, endlessly gesticulating, and their every word and every gesture was like a fresh hammer blow to my head. Finally, they summoned this squat doctor from the second floor who started to feel and examine my head. Then he said to us, half in broken Russian, half in German: "She needs to *machen* x-ray, *machen* encephalograph!" "She doesn't need to *machen* anything," Misha shouted back at him. "She has a migraine! She needs to *machen* an injection!" This plump German then pronounced such a complicated diagnosis that Misha bit his lip, turned pale and said: "Saska! Now I'm going to kill them all!" The plump doctor retorted: "I think you hit woman on head... It is Russian dialogue..."

With the help of the kind German couple, Misha somehow managed to convince the Spaniards to give me an injection. Half an hour later, we left to return to the hotel. Misha said to me in the car: "In comparison with Georgians, Spaniards are just deaf and dumb. Just in case, I nicked a syringe and ampoule off them." He spent the rest of the day looking after me as well as he could. But he was a real butterfingers. Misha once again demonstrated that he had no practical skills. I reminded him of a time in Riga when I had caught awful tonsillitis and had a temperature above 39 Celsius. Ida and Robert were not at home. My temperature fell sharply all of a sudden and I started to shiver horribly. I said to him: "Mishanka! Turn the gas hub on, put the kettle on to boil and make me a hot water bottle." And he looked at me in fright, wringing his hands: "Saska, I don't know how to turn the gas on."

So there we were in Malaga, and I asked him: "Since we separated have you at least learnt how to turn the gas on?" "You're going to laugh, but no!"

The next morning, I felt a bit better and we descended to breakfast. Misha introduced me as his "Saska" to all the tournament players, many of whom were young and whose names I didn't recognize.

I feel sad recalling that time in Malaga. We treated each other as we had done in the early days of our life together. I washed his lucky shirt in his hotel room every day. He refused to wear any other, and it does seem that his shirt brought him luck in that tourney. He was in a great mood. He won the tournament, and after the closing ceremony he said to me: "You were right. I was world champion only with you. You always brought me luck. See? I came first."

His words had a subtext, though. Whenever we had a big row in Riga, I would say to him quite acerbically: "You were world champion only with me! Without me you will never be world champion again!" That was pretty harsh on my part, actually.

If I could live my life again I would not say that to him this time around.

After Malaga, I asked myself one question, one that I continue to ask to this day: had I found an excuse, could we have got back together? I guess not. I just can't imagine how it would have worked. The distance between us was too great. I was lonely but free, and that was something I clung onto. Moreover, he had hurt me far too much. A repeat of our life together would have been a farce. Evidently, Misha also evaluated the situation sensibly. Maybe that is why, when we bid each other our goodbyes, he said nothing else. He just smiled sadly, as though to apologize.

The time machine had tempted us back to the sweet past, but then cold-bloodedly and without emotion dumped us in the present, having made us realize that we were two very close people who had wounded each other. And there was nothing to do other than to acknowledge that as the truth.

I said earlier that, back in Berlin, my friend Vida Vaitkute made every effort to drag me out of my depressive state. She would invite me over and from time to time introduce me to various "respectable men". Her purpose was obvious, yet I was indifferent to these "candidates". Some of them were very sweet, some were businesslike and well-fed Jewish men with short, fat fingers. They had drummed up some sort of "business" – sold or re-sold goods. Actually, this word "business" was somewhat ugly to me. My Soviet upbringing made itself felt and I associated the word with a somewhat dishonest, underground and dirty activity. Of course, I was wrong – many of them were perfectly decent without any hint of impropriety. But at the time, they were all the same as each other to me, each with short, fat fingers. It was a sort of neurosis I suffered from!

Well, a little later, Vida introduced me to her friend Eva. Eva suggested going on a tour of Belgium for a week. Her friends met us in Antwerp. They were a family who owned a large jewelry shop. They invited over other friends the day we arrived. In Europe, they are fond of these casual parties. Eva, naturally, sat me at the piano. I don't know what impression I made on people at the party, but one lady clung onto me the whole evening, telling me about this exquisite man called Joe Kramarz, about how clever and charming he was, and how she would love to introduce me to him. "He's a businessman, does he have short, fat fingers?" I asked. "Oh, what are you talking about!" she replied totally seriously to my attempt at irony. "He's an amazing man! The whole of Belgium is in love with him!"

You win some, you lose some. Three days later, I was invited to somebody else's house, and Joe Kramarz was one of the guests. I played the piano and sang both uplifting and sad little ditties from my repertoire of my past career. Joe appeared to be a thoroughly decent guy. He spoke rarely, but with wit. Above all, I was struck by his amazingly wise, penetrating and kind eyes. He looked about 55, but, as it later transpired, was much older, and the gap between us was 27 years.

Oh, and his fingers were long and aristocratic...

I liked him as a person. And it seemed that he liked me, too. At least, when we sat down to eat, he said: "I will sit down on one condition: after dinner, Sally will play the piano again." During dinner, Joe's friend, who had invited him to the party, told him: "Joe, I believe that you've preferred chess to business your entire life." "Yes," Joe replied, "I can't hide the fact that were I able to make a living from chess I would have given up everything else." His friend continued, now turning to me: "You see, Sally, Joe is a grandmaster of watches of every imaginable kind, but more than anything else he loves chess. If you ever find yourself back in Antwerp and ask anybody in the street where to find Joe Kramarz, you will hear the reply 'Kramarz is playing chess at the stock exchange.'" "I know all about that," I replied. "Do you like chess, too?" asked Joe all animated. "No, I replied, but I know people who are crazy about it." Then his friend immediately picked up the conversation: "Imagine that, Joe, Sally was Mikhail Tal's first wife."

Joe nearly fell out of his chair: "You were the wife of my idol, my God?" After that, I would often joke with him: "Be honest with me, did you only marry me because I was Tal's wife?" And he would always reply: "The surname Tal isn't of any importance if we are talking about you. Just like the surname Landau." (We talked in German at first, later in French.)

Sometime later, he invited me to travel to the south of France with him. There was no ulterior motive in that, he genuinely wanted to travel to the south of France with me. He behaved impeccably, like a true gentleman, he was sincerely attentive to my needs, and demanded nothing in return. We had a wonderful time. I learnt that Joe was born in Antwerp, but his parents had been Polish Jews. He told me all sorts of things about his life, about his late wife, about his two grown-up sons. I was much less talkative. But he didn't irritate me with any tactless questions.

As we flew back in the airplane, Joe Kramarz asked me to marry him. In this book, which is above all about Misha, I will tell you not only about Joe as a person whom fate gifted me in the second half of my life, but also as a person that Misha adored too, and who became Misha's close friend.

I sold what few possessions I had with me in Berlin and a month later flew back to Antwerp (it took a month for Joe to sort out the required documents).

I officially became Joe Kramarz's wife in December 1981, and in total I lived seven happy years with him. Until his death on 1 June 1988, a month before he would have turned 77, and just two months before my father died (on 9 August). Actually, my father's death is worth recalling here – I was unable to attend his funeral because the Soviet consulate in Belgium refused to grant me a visa. At that funeral, though, Misha despite only being my father's ex son-in-law ignored convention by standing up and delivering the first toast. He proclaimed that he had loved my father dearly, and this was because he had loved, still loved and would always love, his daughter Saska.

Five years after I married Joe, Misha said to me: "I know why God gifted you this treasure. He is a reward for all the pains that I caused you." Misha adored Joe from the first time they met. It was in Merano in 1981, during the Karpov vs. Korchnoi match. It was Joe who persuaded me to go to Merano so that he could be introduced to Misha. I didn't require much convincing and we left for Italy. It was our honeymoon, only in reverse order. As my Jewish luck would have it, I caught a chill in the train, arrived in Merano with a temperature and immediately took to my bed in the hotel. I told Joe to go to the match, find Tal and introduce himself as my husband-to-be. Joe did exactly that and they got chatting. Upon returning, Joe told me beaming that his greatest wish had been fulfilled – he had met Tal!

"How did Misha react to the fact that you are my future husband?" I asked.

"He said that he's happy," Joe replied, "but he didn't sound it."

"He's extremely jealous."

"That's hardly surprising. In his place I would be as well."

Misha made an amazing impression on Joe.

"He's a true genius!" Joe kept repeating.

Two days later, Joe got a phone call from Antwerp about problems at his shop. He flew back, but I remained in the hotel. Misha came to my room every day, along with his friend, an oncologist by the surname Gershanovich. They brought me some medicines the first day. He told me a lot about my parents, with whom he was in constant contact, about Gelya, Zhannochka and, of course, about Gera. Gera was fine, and by that time he had married his beloved Nadia. Misha gave them his apartment on the seaside to live in. The Minister had worked hard so that Gera was allowed to resume his university education. However, Misha was naturally focused, above all, on Joe. I portrayed Joe to him in the best light possible. Misha told me: "That's fantastic, Saska! That's what you really deserve! The most important thing is that he's no worse than me." "The most important thing is that Gelya is better than me," I replied.

I felt better after a week and flew to Antwerp, unfortunately without having actually made it to the match. I gave Misha Joe's contact details. "I'll bombard you two with calls," Misha warned. He did indeed call us frequently in Antwerp, and from everywhere. After chatting to me he would always ask to put Joe on the line. And if I told him that I felt well, Misha would always ask Joe whether I really did feel well.

Joe was an unusually kind man, and in fact he had a lot in common with Misha. For example, like Misha he was indifferent to what he was wearing, what he ate and what furniture stood in his apartment. He made sure to enjoy every second of his life, as though foreseeing that it would end in the not too distant future. If it was sunny in the morning, he would wake me up with: "Sallynka! How can you sleep when there is such a wonderful sun outside?" If it rained, he would be glad, saying: "Sallynka! Just look at that luxurious rain!" Just like Misha, he couldn't understand why I would lie flat out as though mowed down by my migraines." And like Misha, he would rush from corner to corner, trying to alleviate my pains but without the faintest idea how.

Basically, my life had turned out wonderfully, and my only disappointment was that my son wasn't with me. And I also really wanted Misha to get the message that I was doing just ever so fine.

However, life, as in chess, has as many black squares as it has white ones. While in Merano, Misha was told that Robert had died. The year before, in 1980, I had found out about Yasha's death while I was in Berlin. "Saska," Misha said to me, "I've now lost almost all of my dearest chess pieces." This loss brought him closer to Gera. They became not just father and son, but proper friends. His loss also prompted him to phone me countless times.

Sometimes he had nothing to say: "Mishanka," I would ask, "you phoned yesterday. Has something happened?" "No, nothing," he answered frequently, "everything that was supposed to happen has already happened. I've called you again to say nothing but to listen to you."

Misha and Joe had their first lengthy get-together in Holland. Misha was playing at the Wijk ann Zee tournament and invited us over.

We stayed in the same hotel as the chess players. Misha booked us a room. So the morning after we arrived, Joe and I went to visit Misha in his room. Well, it was full of smoke, with the ash-try overflowing with butts and chess literature lying everywhere. Misha with his eternal cigarette between his teeth was analyzing a game. Seeing us, he jumped up startled, then started to apologize. And Joe said: "Misha! Stop killing yourself! It's wonderful weather! Let's go for a walk and take breakfast somewhere nice!" Misha looked at him somewhat absently and suggested: "Joe! I have another suggestion: why don't you take a walk, while Saska and I have an innocent chat."

Joe was a most tactful person. He replied that it was a super idea and he left for a walk. Meanwhile, Misha veritably interrogated me: how was I? was I happy? how did Joe treat me? Then we talked about Gera, then about my parents, and I asked whether he could help me visit the USSR to see them. Misha replied that these were troublesome times and the chances were low. So then I asked whether Gera would be able to come and visit me in Antwerp — I had tried to invite him earlier, but to no result. Misha thought for a minute and said that he would try but he doubted it was possible. Then he smiled and said: "How about you tell me about yourself instead?" "I've already told you everything!" I replied. "That's not enough, tell me again!"

Misha and Joe soon became good friends in Holland and started to address each other by the familiar "du" if they spoke in German (they spoke sometimes in German, sometimes in English). Whenever Misha was available, Joe wouldn't leave his side. He reminded me of a happy child whose famous Dad had generously taken him for a walk — even though Joe was much older than Misha. His face glowed with contentment and pride when Misha was surrounded by fans asking for his autograph or telling him how much they admired him. Joe felt Misha's glory as though it were his own. After Holland, we started to meet more often, in fact it became a sort of tradition. Misha would call and invite us to every tourney in Europe where he played. We weren't able to attend all of them, but we managed to visit him in Holland, France and Spain.

I recall one of our last days in Wijk ann Zee. We ate at the hotel restaurant and were getting ready to go to bed, as it was late. Then Misha suddenly ran up to the grand piano, opened the cover, approached me and gallantly led me to it. "Play something," he asked. "It's so long since you played a song for me." So I performed my favorite sentimental song *Autumn bids goodbye with kisses*.

> *Autumn bids goodbye with kisses*
> *On mountain-ashes' lips deep red.*
> *Why did you make me promises*
> *When our love was already dead?*

After finishing, I closed the cover and said: "I played and sang better in Riga." I cannot describe the expression on his face. Misha hugged me and said very quietly: "I'm so lucky that I had, have and will have my Saska." And then he left for his room. Joe, not knowing Russian, obviously understood nothing of what he said and asked me to explain. "Nothing important," I replied, "we were just reminiscing about some inconsequentialities from our life."

I repeat, Misha really liked Joe and treated him like a brother would treat the husband of his favorite sister. Yet at the same time, he always acted as though he had first "priority" over me. Whenever we went to visit him, Misha would stealthily distance Joe from us, take me by the arm, caress me, kiss me and tell me how much he loved me, as though there were no Joe. This of course pained Joe, although he tried not to show it. One day, he said to me: "Misha has probably forgotten that he's no longer your husband and that I'm your husband now." But actually, Misha hadn't forgotten, and nor did he want to offend Joe: he was simply being himself and he genuinely believed that nobody in the world had priority above him in relations with "his Saska".

I also remember we went to the chess olympiad in Lucerne in 1982 and Joe said to me in wonder: "Look how many great grandmasters have come to Lucerne. And I'm not just talking about Karpov and Kasparov... Yet it's Tal that everybody is running after." That was absolutely true.

Once, we agreed with Misha to go all three of us together to a restaurant after a game. However, the game got to the end of the session and was adjourned. Misha found a place in the press-center to carry out his analysis. After eleven p.m., I said to Joe that it was getting late and that we should postpone dinner with Misha until the next day. We went to bed. Then there was a knock on the door after midnight. I opened it and Misha walked in. "We agreed to go for dinner. Get dressed! I'll be waiting for you and Joe in the restaurant!" "Mishanka!" I replied. "It's past midnight! Don't be silly!" "Then wake up Joe, let's chill out in your room!"

At three a.m., Joe said: "Misha! I had two dreams in my life. The first has come true. Thanks to Sally, I met you. But I had another dream – to play a game against the greatest player of the twentieth century..." Misha: "I was born to turn your fairytale into reality!" Joe pulled out a chess board and they sat down to play. Joe was quite excited. His cheeks burned bright. He hunched over the board, thought long over his moves and breathed heavily after making each one. Meanwhile, Misha turned away from the board and made his moves almost without looking, humming opera tunes and from time to time teasing Joe for his moves. They played five or six games and the result was predictable. Before he left, Misha whispered to me generously: "He doesn't play as badly as I hoped. But he isn't going to become world champion. Then again, nor am I."

One day in Paris, Misha was set to play a simultaneous exhibition on 33 boards, and so Joe asked to be number 34. Misha, naturally, didn't object. He won thirty games, drew three and lost one. Joe was one of the thirty defeated and wasn't happy:

"I don't understand how I lost to him. I had a completely drawn position. Why couldn't he have offered me a draw?"

I then say to Misha: "Couldn't you have let Joe draw? He's such a wonderful man, why didn't you afford him that little bit of pleasure?"

"I really wanted to beat him," said Misha laughing. "It was revenge for my defeat. After all, he won you off me... Now, as the winner I will send Joe off to bed, while you will come and sit in my room until I leave for the airport."

But Misha didn't always tease Joe. Sometimes, he would take him under his wing...

In Brussels, Misha invited us to lunch. We found a pretty little restaurant, the sort where you weren't forced to hand your coat to the cloak-room attendant upon entry. I hung my coat on the back of my chair. As I got up to leave, Misha sprang up to offer me my coat. Joe had missed this trick and I rebuked him: "Joe, at your age it's about time to learn to hold a coat for a lady." "But at your age," Misha retorted, "it's time for you to forget it."

The longer I lived in emigration the more I wanted to go and visit the Soviet Union. I wasn't tormented by nostalgia. I didn't dream of the little streets in Vilnius or Riga, and I had no regrets. But that was where my parents, my son and, ultimately, Misha all lived. I was really worried about their futures. I was worried that they could experience trouble because of me. Maybe I was being over-emotional and exaggerating. Maybe... Yet there was an objective reality at the same time: the KGB and mass media cultivated among Soviet people a quite specific attitude towards emigrants. I found it difficult to come to terms with the reasonable probability that I would never see Gera or my parents again. It was frightening: to know that they lived just a two-hour flight away and yet not to have the chance of even

fleeting contact. Yeah, in those days people said their goodbyes
on the assumption that it was *forever!* As though they were
departing this world. But for as long as a person is alive, they
have hope.

I continued to hope, and I sent invitations to my son
and parents to come and visit me. Moreover, Joe, seeing
my suffering, insisted that I apply to the Soviet consulate in
Antwerp to request a visitor's visa. So in 1983 I showed up there.
I have never been as humiliated as I was that day. They didn't
let me speak with the senior staff. Just a lowly functionary. A
pawn. And an unabashed anti-Semite. When I showed him my
Belgian passport the official took one look at it and said: "It says
here that you're Belgian, but in your old Soviet passport it said
that you are Jewish. You will never be allowed back and you will
never see you parents or your son again! I promise you. You knew
what you were doing." I returned home totally crushed and told
Joe. He got furious, grabbed the phone and started dialing the
number of the Belgian foreign ministry. It took a huge effort,
but I talked him out of it, for fear of the consequences for my
loved ones.

I was eventually allowed to visit in 1987, thanks to the
political changes brought by Mikhail Gorbachev. Joe and I
obtained invitations that year, and I think that Misha's help
was also important. However, I was fated never to enjoy perfect
happiness – shortly after our marriage, Joe was diagnosed with
lymphatic cancer. I was told that even the best medicines would
do no more than prolong his life. Then, very soon after, he
received another diagnosis – rectal cancer – and was urgently
operated on. This was followed by chemo, radio and endless
tests. That went on for several years, on and off, until his death.
He conducted himself bravely and with amazing dignity. After
the first dose of chemo, Joe felt better and insisted on going to

the Lucerne olympiad. "I'm desperate to see Misha again," he said. So we went.

In Lucerne, Misha introduced Joe to Karpov, Roshal, Sosonko and Smyslov. We would often take walks together, and once Smyslov said to him: "Joe, you are so lucky: you have such a charming wife. I think that in losing Sally, Misha lost himself." I tried to disagree, but Smyslov told me: "Dear Sally, when men speak, women are only allowed to take a quiet walk at a distance."

So, we made it to the Soviet Union in 1987. Misha insisted that we meet in Leningrad, as he was playing a tournament there. We turned up with tons of presents for everybody. I was overjoyed to see at last Gera, his wife, my wonderful granddaughters, Gelya, Zhannochka, Mum and Dad.

Misha took Joe with him to every game. Joe was already suffering badly by then, but only he knew that. He even said to Misha: "I know damn all about medicine, and the doctors take advantage of me to make me buy expensive medicines and undergo complex examinations. They are pumping my entire wealth out of me." Misha replied: "It's the same story with me."

Joe was taken aback by how many cigarettes Misha smoked, "and he drinks one too many... he's killing himself," Joe complained. "He doesn't have the right to think only about himself! He will leave the whole of civilization an orphan!" Misha already looked worse for wear in Leningrad. But if, in the past, his exotic appearance could be considered part and parcel of his genius on the back of his phenomenal results, then by 1987, when the fanfares were just a memory, when he was tired of his illnesses and had aged, when new, young, trendily dressed chess players had appeared on the scene, Tal was now a pitiful sight to behold. Did Misha realize this? I think that he did. Once after I yelled at him for his carefree attitude to his health and external appearance, he replied sadly: "Saska, I am totally aware of all that. There will be no more pleasant surprises to come. I'm playing out a hopeless endgame. But I hope that I can make just a little more mischief. There's no time left for a return match. I'm just going to wing it until I get checkmated."

As I wrote earlier, Misha was close to the oncologist Dr. Gershanovich, and he asked him in Leningrad to examine Joe. Gershanovich looked over Joe and then told me one-on-one: "Sally, must I tell you the truth?" "Yes, only the truth!" I replied. "Joe's heart is in great shape, and he's a very strong, resilient guy. So I will give him five years to live." However, it was Misha to whom he actually told the truth: Joe wouldn't last more than a year...

I was of course fully aware that Joe was terminally ill, yet I found it impossible to accept. That's just human nature: subconsciously, without any logic, one continues to hope. To pin hopes on some hidden reserves in the body, on the life-giving strength of new medicines, on prayers even. And in a totally hopeless situation one still looks for a miracle. I couldn't imagine the day that Joe would no longer be with me. I stubbornly refused to believe that fate, which had gifted me such peace and happiness in the second half of my life, was now going to take it all away. After Joe's health worsened I tried not to leave him alone for a minute, and I kept waiting for him to get better. I kept thinking he would go into remission and get out of his hospital bed and we would set off travelling again, to the sea, to Misha's next tournament – and then I would calm down. And I would gradually convince myself that he really would get better, that God had heard me. I would draw up fun plans for the future, for five years' hence, for ten years' hence...

But just as I did, that same cold, callous thought from deep inside would come to the surface: what five years am I talking about? What ten years? The day when he was no longer with me would arrive soon, very soon...

After that, an optimistic, calming thought would again replace all that: stop talking nonsense! Everything will be fine! There is a higher justice!

Misha and I held a long conversation about Joe, about me, and he asked me to treat the situation seriously. "Saska," he said, "Joe's situation is beyond hope. Sadly, he is going to die. You need to get used to the fact that you will lose him. Think about yourself, about your health. Think about the future." I don't recall Misha ever being as serious as that. *But now, when I think about it, when talking about Joe, he was really talking about himself.*

Gershanovich wasn't wrong in his one-year prognosis. Joe spend his last months in his bed at home. He had had enough of hospital. By now, morphine failed to relieve his terrible pain, and only served to dull his awareness.

Once, shortly before his death, I went into his bedroom. He suddenly opened his eyes, and said: "You always loved to spend New Year in Italy, in Spain. To spend Pesach in Israel. And instead you are wasting all your energy to keep me on Earth for one more day. Don't make yourself suffer any more. Let me go. You are young and beautiful. You will find a good man. And I've made provisions to look after you. I also know that only you will come and visit my grave."

Joe died one fine, sunny day. That evening, Misha phoned me from the Soviet Union. His call was very supportive. He comforted me as much as he could, and at the end of our conversation told me: "My poor thing, I know how much you are suffering, but remember just this: your Miska is always with you and he is bursting with strength and health."

Gera had come to visit me for the first time in Belgium at that time. He made a huge effort to extend his stay for a few days to help me bury Joe. Then we held the shiva, where a huge number of people showed up. Gera looked after me and attended to the guests, while I just sat there, my mind numbed with tranquillizers. Once Gera and I eventually found ourselves alone, I said to him: "There we are, my son, my life is over. I'm already 49, there won't be another guy like Joe, and all the others will only come dancing around my money, like a moth around a light." Gera jumped up, ran around the room in a way that reminded me of Misha, and half-shouted: "How can you say that! God bequeathed you the ability to love and to be loved! And he won't let you down! And nobody but God can take what is yours by right away from you! You are alive, and that means I am there for you and so is Dad!"

After Joe's death I couldn't find my place in life. Antwerp seemed to me to be dead and empty. I couldn't remain in the apartment for long. I suffered insomnia, and in those short moments when I managed to doze off Joe would appear in my dreams and beg me to go to Italy with him. The dreams seemed so real that upon waking up my first desire was to pack my suitcase for the upcoming journey. It was torture. I thought I was going mad.

Joe of course left me enough to live on. I was now the owner of some properties. But I was a totally useless businesswoman. I had barely tried to manage the estate when this artful Greek spiv pulled a fast one on me. I was told in court that even if they caught him and I won the case, I wouldn't get any money back as he didn't have any — he had registered all his property to people just fronting for him and the only consolation I would get would be to see him jailed. Since then, I have stopped trying to actively administer anything.

I don't know how I would have coped with these disasters if it wasn't for Misha.

One day, he phoned me to say that he would spend a couple of days in Paris on his way to a tournament in Spain. He told me to drop everything and head for Paris without a moment's thought.

"Firstly, I want to see you," he said, "and secondly, Paris is a city where you let go of all the bad things and acquire good things, including me."

Misha appeared, as always, at just the right time. I had just put together a set of documents required for Gera's emigration from the USSR. There wouldn't be a more secure chance to hand over the papers. I went to meet him at Charles de Gaulle airport, waiting by the arrivals exit. Passengers began to emerge, and among them I noticed an elderly man with an ill-looking face. He was wearing an old-fashioned coat and a Soviet-style worker's cap that was far too big for him. It wasn't easy to make out in him the brilliant darling of the fans, the famous Mikhail Tal. Yet it was him. Misha looked so damned awful that I took fright. He was totally sober, yet I just caught the smell of his favorite Martell. He reacted instantly to my scared look and laughed: "Don't worry, Ginger! I'm just rehearsing for the role of Mikhail Tal the scarecrow in a new comedy." "Misha," I replied, "this is no comedy. It's a horror film!" He hugged me and continued: "The horror film would have happened if you hadn't come to meet me."

Misha told me about Gera, asked how I was doing and really blossomed when the conversation turned to Zhanna. Two days later, I saw him off at the airport. He was in a jovial mood and told me that after those two days he hadn't felt better in ages. Meanwhile, I had only one thought: how on Earth could he play chess in such a monstrous state?

He phoned me a week later. "Saska, it seems I'm beginning to play pretty good chess!"

...The bright sun of glory shined above the young champion, his future appeared joyful and cloudless... But God determined otherwise, and Tal came to face a number of painful trials. His later creative and sporting career was darkened by serious kidney problems accompanied by sharp, unbearable pains. His bouts of illness would appear unexpectedly, often during competitions. The only surprise was that after so many operations under general anesthetic Misha retained amazing clarity and quickness of thought.

His illness was incurable. The doctors saw perfectly well that Tal's days on Earth were numbered. Yet a miracle happened: Tal continued to bravely resist this terminal ailment for several years. Chess was the medicine that kept him going! Whenever his illness took a step back, Misha immediately dived into the crucible of chess battle...

Viktor Malkin, Doctor of Medicine, *Shakhmatny Vestnik,* 1992

I then met Misha in Brussels, to where he had flown with Gelya. This was after two stomach operations in Riga, after he had suffered internal bleeding whose reason the doctors were unable to identify even during the ops. Misha was very weak and his legs could hardly move. Gelya obviously couldn't let him travel by himself. At Gelya's request, a doctor in Antwerp whom I knew examined Misha in the hotel and found an abscess around a stich. He said this was probably caused by a reaction to the threads that the doctors had forgotten to remove. He said it would probably have to be punctured, and this was actually done later.

What shocked me the most was that after the examination, when he was in an awful state, Misha insisted that we all go to a restaurant(!). There, he ordered shellfish and eels — all pretty spicy — drank several shots of spirit and spent the entire dinner spraying jokes about the sophistication of humanity, which had managed to figure out that all these ugly-looking sea creatures were actually the most refined delicacies. The doctor grabbed his head, sure that he would need to call for an ambulance. Yet Misha's constitution was a mystery! That said, he only managed to play two or three games in the tourney before withdrawing.

In January 1990, Gera and his family emigrated to Israel. I immediately went to visit, as did Misha, Gelya and Zhanna. Everybody was in a great and carefree mood — for the first time in three years, we all got together at the dinner table as one big family.

Misha was on form, his usual witty self. He ate and drank heartily, and kept running out of the room for a smoke. We all had the impression that he was beginning to shed his ailments.

Gera took many photos of that visit, which we developed after Misha left. One day, Gera and I were sitting on the couch viewing them when he suddenly jumped up with alarm in his voice and exclaimed: "Mum, look! This isn't our Dad! This is an old, dead man!" I felt ill at his words, but they ringed true.

For as long as Misha was with us, he emitted some sort of magic aura that made him seem young and healthy to those around him. But in the photos he was a colorless shadow of the man who had once been Misha Tal — joyless, without the slightest spark in his eyes. Like a magnificent Christmas tree whose garlands of lights were suddenly switched off.

Having spent my entire adult life with Misha in one form or another, I often witnessed the effects of his suddenly "switching off" — but they were different effects this time and had a different cause. In the past, he would "switch off" when he ceased to find the conversation interesting. His conversation partner would as a rule notice this, and what happened subsequently would depend on the latter's tact. "Switching off" meant one thing: "I'm sorry, I'm out of time." A tactful person would take this opportunity to end the conversation and stop talking. Or would even leave. Whereas a tactless person needed to have it spelt out to them. Sometimes it was me who did the explaining, sometimes Koblencs. Or Gelya.

But Misha could also "switch on" – as a rule, when the conversation turned to chess. Albeit with the condition that his conversation partner knew something about the game. Experts could chat to each other for hours, sprinkling the conversation with an unbelievable number of their own quotes or those of other people. Chess players talk to each other in the language of notation. I was always amazed at this. Although I understood nothing of it, I listened to them as though they were aliens, observing their emotions. If, for example, Tal, Stein and Gufeld got together, their conversation could flow along the following lines:

Gufeld: What would you say to knightdfourfsixbishopg2?

Stein: Bishopgsevenfgknightdefivecheck!

Tal: Yes but you've forgotten about if knightfsixintermezzoqueenheight!

Gufeld: Queenheightrookgeightwithcheckandrooktakes height and you're left without your mummy!

Tal: But after bishopeone you're left without your daddy!

Stein: Bishopeone doesn't work because of the obvious knighttakeseonecfourdekinggsevenrookasevencheck!

And this wonderful chitchat would continue endlessly, with people not "in-the-know" thinking they were in a mad-house.

...All the young players, while fervently respecting Geller, Polugaevsky and Tal, were ready to refute each and every one of them at the board. And that's wonderful. That was how our generation treated Botvinnik, Bronstein and Keres...

...The other side of the problem was advanced not so much by the young players themselves but by their so-called fans. Again, you have to bear in mind that there are different sorts of fans. Back in 1960, in the Pushkin Theater in Moscow, and again in 1961 in the Entertainment Theater, the majority of fans supported me, not Botvinnik. They wanted something new, something fresh! I'm sure that if I were to play a match against Anatoly Karpov now that same majority would root for him. It's a law of nature and you can't do anything about it. It's only unpleasant when they make these frank generalizations to fit their desired results: "these older players" (meaning they have no prospects, no hope). In truth, what will be will be. We don't plan to offer any gifts. We will make way, but only over the chess board. Unlike others, I have no intention of ruining my relations with those who outplay me. But may they first outplay me all by themselves.

Mikhail Tal, *64*, 1979

Misha also "switched on" if the conversation turned to soccer. He was a huge soccer fan and often dragged me along to matches during our travels. I could never understand what all this hysteria was about: just as Misha couldn't teach me to play chess, he couldn't make me passionate about soccer. He eventually stopped asking me to join and would tell his friends: "Saska watches the game like a sheep watches the goal posts!"

Sometimes, Misha's "switching ons" involved cards. He especially enjoyed belote, which he had learnt from Robert, as well as bridge. I once told him that ladies in Antwerp wanted to teach me bridge. Misha replied: "Saska! It's even more complicated than chess. You'd find learning Japanese easier!"

Another reason why I'm writing these fragments from my memories is to show how Misha had all sorts of passions.

That day when we were pouring over the photos with Misha, Gera said to me: "I can't persuade Dad to come back to Israel, if not forever, then at least for treatment." "My son," I said, "it's pointless. They offered to treat him in Switzerland, Canada, France... Just about everywhere! But your Dad likes only one country, the Soviet Union!"

Here too, Misha was an extraordinary person. I know that he was given direct and indirect invitations to go and live in a number of countries. But he refused to countenance such ideas. Once, he said to me: "Even if I took offense at the entire Soviet Union ten times more than Korchnoi I still wouldn't go and live anywhere else." But he never condemned anybody – neither those who left, nor those who chose to remain. He understood perfectly well the financial and political motivations of the emigrants.

Misha made arrangements so that Gelya and Zhannochka would spend most of their time while he was alive in Germany, at the home of his friend and fan, an old German professor. The idea was for Zhannochka, who had suffered various ailments since birth, to be fed and treated properly and to focus on music. Not long before Misha died, Alik Bakh told him: "You don't look after yourself. Think what will happen with Gelya and Zhannochka if something happens to you." Misha replied: "Don't worry, they will be taken care of."

Gelya and Zhannochka now live in Germany. We call each other often. As for Gera, he's always their dear guest.

Misha knew the price of everything, but he cared neither for money nor politics. He always stayed true to himself, a man from another world. Once when I still lived in Riga, he said to me: "Saska, my feet have been hurting all day, since this morning, and I can't figure out why." I glanced at his legs and burst out laughing. He was wearing two different shoes, both of them for his right feet. I think that he would have even walked around Monte Carlo in worn out shoes.

There are people who specially cultivate for themselves the image of a "genius", and for some reason they believe that the biggest sign of genius is eccentricity and absent-mindedness. I know people like that, but Misha wasn't one of them. He really was a genius, and really was absent-minded. Some geniuses have no ambition. Misha, however, was ambitious. He loved being at the center of attention and tried to be so. This energized him and spurred him on. It happens in the acting world, too: the actor loves it when the theater is overflowing with fans. At the same time, Misha never tried to gain attention artificially. He never acted up, never did anything specially to that aim, never spent time perfecting his hair-style in front of the mirror.

Fragment of an interview with chess master Evgeny Bebchuk

E.B.: Mr. Tal, you are now fifty years old! It seems impossible to believe...

Tal: Yeah, I find it hard to believe too, when I'm not looking in the mirror! When you're twenty you think you will always be twenty, and suddenly another thirty pass...

E.B.: Nevertheless, Tal remains Tal! You are still one of the strongest players in the world. And your popularity is even higher, everybody recognizes you everywhere.

Tal: Something odd happened to me quite recently: I went on a trip to the city of Lipetsk, entered a cafe to have dinner and heard one guy at the next table tell his buddy: "Look, he's the spitting image of Tal!" His buddy replied: "The resemblance is striking, but that guy is dumber and older." Seriously, though, I like being among people, I spend a lot of my time touring with lectures and simuls. And I think that thousands of chess fans know I do. So our love is mutual...

E.B.: What's your attitude to the fact that the battle for the chess crown has transposed from an individual battle to one between entire teams backing each player?

Tal: It's a shame. According to Flohr, Alekhine once rebuked him for actively helping Euwe in their 1935 match. Flohr then said to himself, "a professional grandmaster shouldn't interfere in the duel of others," so two years later he chose not to assist Euwe.

I think that any player contesting the world championship match needs to have a person by their side who has supported them over the years. For Botvinnik that was Rogozin and, later, Goldberg. I had Koblencs, Petrosian had Boleslavsky. Today, there is Karpov who has worked with Zaitsev for many years, while Kasparov has Nikitin... I don't think it right to create large teams.

E.B.: Let's return to how chess has changed... Remember you said a few years ago that "today I would have destroyed the old Tal"? You were referring to Tal the world champion. So does that mean that you currently play chess better?

Tal: The overall level of masters and grandmasters has risen. My statement then, and my repeating it right now, is based on the fact that in the intervening years I (and this goes for others too, of course) have gained more experience and some of the moves that I played in 1959-1960 look ridiculous today.

E.B.: As a person endlessly devoted to chess, what do you dream of?

Tal: I dream that we will be able to travel to Moscow, show up at the central chess club... Chess will reign supreme there, and we will be able to argue about purely chess problems until we get hoarse. Today we are called upon to speak frankly — so I've been frank with you. After that, there won't be any more in-groups, and people will end their petty (and, forgive me, often stupid) resentments at each other. And there will be a notice in the entrance hall that says, for example: "Grandmaster Tal will deliver a lecture today entitled What I did for chess*", and the kids will come to the club and see a teacher in every master and grandmaster, a person they cannot afford to ignore as a role model.*

Shakhmatny Vestnik, 1986

I remember during the first match with Botvinnik that we decided to go for a meal in the restaurant Aragvi. There was a sizeable queue to get in, fifty or sixty people. We joined the queue at the back. Delicious aromas wafted from the restaurant, and Misha said: "Saska! You're going to play the next game against Botvinnik. On my behalf. Because I'm dying of hunger." "Misha," I suggested, "let's go to the entrance and say that you're Mikhail Tal. They'll let us in straight away." "I'm not comfortable doing that," he replied. "If you're not comfortable, die of hunger." But then a man standing in front of us turned around and exclaimed with a Georgian accent: "Look. It's our Mikho! Mikho Tal!" The crowd instantly parted and we were literally carried into the restaurant. Misha was quite embarrassed and blushed, but I could see that he was enjoying it.

On the other hand, he was sometimes capable of the most incredible feats. During the return match with Botvinnik, Misha and I were invited to a circus show where the famous clown Oleg Popov was performing. The administrator gave us a formal welcome, while the walrus trainer said that he would invite Tal into the ring in the second act to perform an easy trick with the walruses. Misha lit up like a child.

However, at the end of the first act he was struck down with almighty pains. During the break, we were accompanied backstage and they called an ambulance. Misha was given an injection and we were taken back to the hotel. Yet the next day, Misha was back playing Botvinnik.

Once I got the chance to peek backstage at the actor and standup comedian Arkady Raikin. He wasn't young by then and had already survived two heart attacks. In the dressing room, an elderly-looking and ill man, speaking and moving with difficulty, had just sat down. Yet he emerged on stage and was instantly transformed as though by magic. Here he was like in years past, a young and brilliant artist who moved around easily on stage as though dancing, gesticulating, delivering lengthy monologues. It seemed like time held no power over him. I was struck by this phenomenon in Misha, too. From where did he get his crazy energy? Where in his worn out, ill body, nested this inexplicable life force and implacable desire to fight at the chess board? He spent his last two years with a temperature constantly around 38 Celsius and a staph infection in his blood. Yet he continued to play! In classic tournaments, in blitz tournaments. And he was even among the leaders... In 1988, Mikhail Tal became world blitz champion! No, it wasn't for nothing that they said of Misha: "Tal will always be Tal!"

Fragment of an interview with chess master Evgeny Gik
E.G.: Did you never regret devoting your entire life to chess?
Tal: Chess is my world. It's not a home, not a fortress where I hide away from life's worries, but an entire world. A world where I live life to the full, where I express myself. I love the atmosphere of matches and tournaments, of chess-related discussions. I can't imagine myself on an uninhabited island without a chess board and pieces, without an opponent. Well, Friday would have to play a match of a thousand games against me. I don't like to play behind closed doors. I love the public, the noise from the audience doesn't

affect me. When the fans begin to murmur after I make a move, I get inspired – I know that I've played something interesting.

But the chess world isn't a closed one for me. It has many ties to other worlds. Most of my friends aren't grandmasters and are unlikely to become them. But I have a common language with each of them. Yet my other passions – the theater, literature, music – they never compete with chess and always give way to it. That's why, despite defeats, failures, strokes of misfortune, I don't regret other promising chances I had, opportunities I declined. I simply enjoy playing chess.

E.G.: What's your understanding of the beauty of chess?

Tal: For many masters, the beauty of chess consists of the triumph of logic. A great game, in their opinion, is a wonderful classical building with perfect proportions in which every element, every brick is in the right place. And although I also gain pleasure from coming out on top in such purely positional duels, I'm fonder of the triumph of illogical irrationality. The board hosts a frenzied battle subordinate to some great idea, all calculated to the finest detail, plans are carried out strictly on time, yet the outcome of the struggle is decided by a knight move in the corner of the board that has nothing to do with the main theme of the drama.

Speaking in the language of mathematics, in chess I love most of all the instant when the cathetus of the triangle is longer than the hypotenuse!

Shakhmatny Vestnik, 1983

Misha had another particularity. Despite all his modesty and his desire not to be pointed at, he was totally uninhibited and relaxed. He often said: "Popular opinion is the opinion of the public, and the public should keep it handy." While we lived together in Riga and enjoyed the luck that had befallen us, he would often goof around. Say a tourney was underway and games were being played on the stage. Silence in the playing hall, and suddenly he would notice me. Jumping over the barrier in a flash, he would run to me and start to kiss me in front of everybody. His mother was constantly in anguish at this strange behavior. "What on Earth are you doing in front of everybody?" she would ask stunned. But Misha would reply: "Murochka, I'm not comfortable kissing somebody else's wife in front of other people, but I'm perfectly comfortable kissing my own! Let everybody watch and envy me!"

He once called me in Antwerp and tried to convince me to return to the USSR. To be close to him. "Mishanka, stop talking nonsense, you must be drunk," I replied. "I'll repeat all this to you tomorrow when I'm sober!" But he didn't call back the next day.

After Misha married Gelya, I stopped worrying about his passions on the side. I could hear something without being offended by it. Once, I phoned Gelya when she and Zhannochka were living in Germany in the house of Misha's friend. I asked: "How is Misha coping there on his own with his pains?" Gelya blurted out: "Don't worry, he's not alone... He tells everybody she's his secretary." To be honest, Misha's passions even today remain a mystery to me. I don't know the woman that Gelya was referring to and I don't want to say anything bad about her. Though I heard that absolutely everybody was in shock at this liaison. Still, the stark truth is that Misha would place even a fleeting passion on a pedestal and would subsequently never say a bad word about her. When I asked him how he could remain with a woman about whom the nastiest stories circulated, he replied: "Saska, but you know that most of all in women I adore kindness! And she is very, very kind."

Gera knew about all this from the very beginning, but he firmly kept this a secret between boys. Only once I tried to raise this topic of conversation with him (a woman's curiosity is insurmountable!). He replied: "Dad has the right to inexplicable impulsions and nobody should criticize him." "But what's your personal opinion?" I asked Gera. "My opinion is just my opinion, and nothing more than that." "Daddy's boy," I thought." Actually, Gera's inherited self-confidence and independence came to the fore on other occasions.

Gera told me that at my father's funeral Misha had praised me with such lofty words that he felt uncomfortable. "I think it was the one and only time that my father was tactless," my son said to me. "Tactless in respect of Gelya, sorry Mum."

Returning to the topic of "male solidarity", I recall one conversation with my father. He possessed an amazing voice, a tenor. When Jewish musical bands, shows and songs became fashionable in Lithuania father sang a lot, and he and my mother made a number of records. He died suddenly from a stroke, five minutes before a concert was due to begin. Misha and my father had special, warm relations. Both when Misha and I were still one family, and after that. They spent time together independently of me, as buddies. During Misha's affair with L. my father, who was in Moscow at the time, encountered Misha by chance in a hotel lift together with L.. My father knew about Misha's affair and didn't react at all. He didn't ask Misha a single question. In fact, he didn't tell me about that encounter either... It was only many years later that he let it slip purely by accident, and I asked him why he had been silent about it all those years. I was his daughter, after all! Dad replied: "If your husband had been a run-of-the-mill womanizer, I would have acted differently. But your husband was Tal! Person Number One! He was allowed to do everything. While you were Person Number Two, and Jupiter is allowed to do things that a bull may not[21]! You have to understand that!"

---

[21] The Russian version of *Quod licet Iovi, non licet bovi*

How Misha found the energy to go chasing skirt remains a complete mystery to me. But I don't have the right to condemn him. Nobody has the right to condemn him.

I still have a letter that Botvinnik sent to me dated 1 November 1967. It's written in Botvinnik's typical school-masterly tone:

Sally,

Perhaps it will be unpleasant for you to read this letter, but I don't see any other way to help Mikhail. Having a pretty good idea of what illness Mikhail is suffering from I chatted with professor A. V. Snezhnevsky. He (Snezhnevsky) is not only the director of the Institute of Psychiatry of the Academy of Medical Sciences but also a man able to distribute many medicines brought from abroad. Snezhnevsky is willing to provide Mikhail with the necessary aid if Mikhail makes an appointment with him in Moscow. If Mikhail comes to Moscow, then, obviously, it would be advisable to bring with him the doctor responsible for treating him, or, at worst, the history of his illness.

If Mikhail is unable to come to Moscow (which I do believe is the fastest way for him to get well), then Snezhnevsky's assistant recommends contacting Grigory Abramovich Rotstein, who is currently a professor at the Riga Medical Institute. Rotstein specializes in just the type of illness that Mikhail evidently suffers from.

All the medicines that Mikhail needs can be sent to Rotstein from Moscow. Without doubt, such medicines are not available in Riga.

According to information that I obtained by chance about Mikhail's health, I suspect that he is not being treated by the latest medicines. These days, such an illness can be treated by fairly tolerable medication.

Kindly write back to Salo Flohr (or me) with your decision.

I hope that you haven't forgotten me.
With sincere regards, M. Botvinnik

I think that Botvinnik had failed to grasp the situation. Just imagine what would have happened had we sent Misha to stay at the Institute of Psychiatry in a secret operation. Tal would have spent the rest of his life branded a mental case and drug addict. That would have automatically rendered him only "partially capable of work" and, therefore, not permitted to travel abroad. At best, he would have eked out a career like a dolphin caught and placed in a dolphinarium.

I showed Botvinnik's letter to Misha. He read it very seriously and then thought about it for a while, staring into space as though trying to recall a forgotten opening line. Then he raised his eyebrows as though something had dawned on him, and exclaimed: "I get it! The Patriarch has fallen in love with you and wants to lure you to Moscow. But why would you want to trade one ex-world champion for another?"

It appeared to be one of Misha's typical jokes, but I'm not sure that this time it was just that. Misha's relations with Botvinnik were complicated. They contained a certain subtext – after all, it wasn't that long since they had been exchanging heavy punches, and that could not have passed without lasting consequences. Still, Misha was of the highest opinion about Botvinnik as a chess player.

Generally, as I wrote earlier, Tal got on well with the entire chess elite (though it may well be that some of them liked him in the same way that Salieri liked Mozart). Misha was on good terms with Borya Spassky, respected and admired Paul Keres, adored Petrosian and was happy like a child when Tigran became world champion. Of the younger generation, he loved Rafik Vaganian. He noticed Kasparov when Garry was still very young. I once asked Misha: "Tell me, is Garik really that gifted?" "He's a genius," Misha replied. I remember Misha taking Lenya Stein's death really badly. He considered Stein to be one of the mostly likely challengers for the world champion's throne. I think I remember everybody, after all, in my time I knew them all well. Although now I find it hard to imagine that all this really happened.

In the last two years of his life, Misha called me particularly often. From all sorts of countries. "Saska, I still haven't seen you since Israel." "Saska, I'm in country X, come and visit." "Saska, I have told you not all the words." I even said to him once: "Mishanka, you could have bought your own airplane with the money you've spent on phone calls." Well, I'm convinced he realized the end was nigh.

His very last phone call was from Germany, from Gelya's home. That call will stay with me until the day I die. He begged me to meet him in Tilburg, pointing out that it was very close to Antwerp. I should just jump into my driver's seat and go. Just some ninety minutes to two hours. However, I'd caught a nasty infection at the time, my eyes badly hurt and were all watery, and there was no way I was capable of driving. I replied: "Misha! You play at Tilburg every year. There will be another Tilburg."

Alas, there wasn't another Tilburg...

Gera came to visit me from Israel at the end of June 1992. I really hoped that he would have a proper holiday and I took him to the seaside resort of Knokke, where I'd rented an apartment for the summer. Upon arrival, we headed straight to the beach without unpacking our bags. We sunbathed for two hours, ate lunch in a little restaurant on the seafront, and returned to the apartment. Gera lay down on the couch and seemed to fall asleep. I also went to lie down, in the other room.

Suddenly, my heart began to beat rapidly and I experienced pangs of alarm. It seems like nature has bequeathed me an inexplicable gift of foreboding. Actually, Misha often commented on it. I got up and started to pace the room, from corner to corner. Grabbed a cigarette and lit it. Then I instinctively went into Gera's room and told him: "We have to go back to Antwerp! We can't stay here any longer!" "What's the matter, Mum?" he asked. I replied: "Something has happened. I don't know what, but something has happened." My state had by now frightened my son, and without saying another word he grabbed the still unpacked bags and we drove straight back to Antwerp, at breakneck speed. I suddenly remembered that Gera had told me during the journey to Knokke about a terrible nightmare he had experienced the night before, and after that I was left in no doubt that *something* had indeed happened!

Everything that happened after that seemed surreal...

The second we crossed the doorway of my apartment in Antwerp I dashed to the answering machine. Gelya was telling the machine right then, in a state of anxiety: "Misha's in a really bad way. Zhannochka and I are flying to Moscow."

I collapsed in the armchair as though thunder-struck.

My heart was jumping out of my chest and I had just one thought in my mind: "This time it won't end happily." Gera was rushing around the apartment in total confusion. He tried to comfort me: "This isn't the first time it's happened to Dad, it'll be all right in the end." But I saw that he was barely composing himself. Gera said that he had to get to Moscow but insisted that I stay at home — he was too worried about me.

Well, it was easy to say that he had to get to Moscow. How was he going to do that? Gera was by then an Israeli citizen and had no Russian visa. "I'm going to the embassy, we'll sort it out there," he said. I learnt later just what efforts he had to make to be accorded a visa.

Gera eventually flew out to Moscow, and I remained alone. I started to phone all the Moscow numbers I knew in order to find out which hospital had him. When I got through at last, I heard just two cruel, ice-cold words: *hopeless situation.* I was unbearably scared in my apartment alone and spent the night at a friend's place.

I tried to focus but couldn't. Thoughts or, more accurately, fragments of thoughts would suddenly appear and disappear without trace. There was just one persistent question that kept revolving in my mind: "What had I done to offend God to make him take away so many of my nearest and dearest in such a short period of time?"

First Joe, then Dad, and now he was taking Misha. Like mountain climbers who were connected by the same rope.

But Misha wasn't going to die. He had already been saved from so many hopeless situations. He was going to survive this time, too. However, my intuition told me: this time they wouldn't save him.

Or maybe everything would be fine in the end? We were basically used to Misha being ill his entire life, and it was he who had taught us to accept his state. He had made us adapt to him: we considered him immortal, that he would live eternally, and couldn't imagine that this eternity would ever end. Well, of course it would end, but only after us.

At the very least, I knew that as long as Misha was alive he would provide me with spiritual support, a sort of ladder that I could descend to reach the sweet, languid, distant past, or on which I could just stand in the present, experiencing peace and confidence from the knowledge that *he* existed, this great Tal, and that this great Tal still remembered me. I could even take a few steps up this ladder and into the future, having no doubt that *he* was also waiting for me in the future, that he would support me and not let me fall.

In this anxious state of not knowing, I barely waited for morning to come before I told my friend: "I can't stay here, I have to return home."

There was a fax waiting for me at home: "Mum! Dad has DIED. You need to get here."

I opened the first aid cabinet and swallowed a dose of tranquillizers. Then I sat down in the armchair and remained there for a few hours, like a mummy.

A phone call stirred me: "Please, you absolutely have to come here. The funeral will be in Riga." I finally grasped the sense of Ratko Knezevic's words.

Actually, I was scared of going. I was scared of seeing Misha dead. I didn't want to see him dead. I didn't have the right to see him dead. In fact, nobody should see him dead. He wouldn't have let anybody see him dead. I didn't care if this happened to anybody else, but not to him.

After that, Gera phoned and told me that he was really scared for me, that I might not bear Misha's funeral.

I guess I must have been quite out of it, because I told myself: "This is some monstrous hoax! Funeral? They've all gone mad! I have to go there and convince everybody that this is just another of Misha's tricks!"

It wasn't Misha lying in the open coffin. It was a different person, who had been badly done up to look like Misha. Yet everybody was bidding him farewell as though saying goodbye to Misha. It was awful. My overworked brain was still expecting Misha to appear out of nowhere and exclaim: "Hey guys, what's up with you? It's not me in the coffin! Stop crying! I've got a game tomorrow!" But Misha didn't appear, while somebody

resembling Misha continued to lie in the coffin and people kept
bidding him farewell, as though he were Misha.

After that, I recall a whole kaleidoscope of real and at the
same time unreal images. I often dream of Misha's funeral,
and when I wake up I can't figure out whether these dreams are
recollections of actual events or whether those events were just
a dream.

There we are, sitting in the Jewish center, holding hands
tightly, as though grabbing onto each other: Gelya, Zhannochka,
Gera and me. Our Misha is gone forever...

Alik Bakh is crying noisily: "Sallynka, how can he have
died?"

Zhenya Bebchuk is trying as hard as he can not to cry, and
whispers instructions to somebody.

I'm wearing dark glasses. They hide my eyes that are swollen
from tears, which can't see anything in any case except for
Misha. No, that's not Misha...

A tall, burly man says to me: "Sally, I didn't recognize you."
It's Volodya Bagirov.

Sasha Zamchuk, who introduced me to Misha, says to me:
"So that's it." He is confused and acting apologetically.

Yasha's woman, now Yasha's widow.

Gipslis... Ratko Knezevic repeating, "Misha's gone" from
time to time.

Koblencs, totally destroyed, pronouncing something or
other half in Yiddish, half in Russian.

Many people I'd never seen before, some I did know but
whom I'd half forgotten, appearing like ghosts from the past.
Lots of people, yet it seemed like too few. And again I'm
thinking that it's not Misha we're burying, because the entire
world should attend Misha's funeral.

Then the coffin is lowered into the grave.

Rachmaninoff, Rachmaninoff, Rachmaninoff. *His* favorite Rachmaninoff, which since that day provokes only one association in me – Misha's funeral.

Then back to the apartment on Gorky Street. It's as though nothing has changed. Another crowd of people. Some people were even playing blitz, trash talking as they did so and recalling Misha's banter. Some people smoking. Just like in old days, except there is no Ida to complain about the smoke and wipe the dust from the portrait of Doctor Nekhemia Tal. Yasha doesn't scurry into his room with his latest "victim". Misha doesn't drop ash on the chess board and doesn't yell at Robert: "Jack! Bring us the ashtray!" Because Ida, Yasha and Robert no longer live in the apartment. And there is no Misha. And they will never appear in the apartment again.

And again it's the four of us left together, like four orphans. And it was Zhannochka's birthday only yesterday.

Gera speaks very warmly of Karpov, who moved mountains to organize the transport of the coffin from Moscow to Riga.

Extract from an interview given by Anatoly Karpov to Boris Dolmatovsky for Shakhmatny Vestnik, 1993

B.D.: Mr. Karpov, what place does Tal occupy in your life?

A.K.: Tal and I were connected by many things. He was my coach during my match with Korchnoi in Baguio. Then, admittedly, he backed Kasparov and even aided him. Had it been anybody else I wouldn't have let it go. But Tal was Tal. It's a great pity that he's left us. He was a fantastic man, and until the end of his life, even when he was quite ill, he played wonderfully well. I should be so lucky.

And again Rachmaninoff, Rachmaninoff, Rachmaninoff...

I returned to Antwerp, where I continue to live today. Misha's death was the start of a new, quite different period in my life. In

his time, Misha unsuccessfully attempted to teach me chess. I
was a hopeless student, but I did learn how the pieces move and
I picked up some of the jargon. So with Misha's death, I can say
that the middle game has transposed into the endgame. And it's
a hopeless endgame.

My mind knows that Misha has gone, yet all this time, as I
wrote earlier, I have this relentless sense that he's somewhere
playing in his latest tournament, but for some reason no
longer phones. I often catch myself waiting for his phone call.
Sometimes, the phone does actually ring, I grab the receiver and
hear: "Ginger?" Misha's vocal intonations and those of our son
are remarkably similar. Sometimes uncomfortably so.

But I no longer hear the familiar "Saska!" Even Gelya, who
when Misha was alive also called me "Saska", now only calls me
"Sallynka". "Why not Saska? Why do you call me Sallynka?"
"Sallynka," Gelya replies, "you were Saska for Misha, and,
while he was alive, for me, too. But now you are Sallynka."

Memories frequently merge into my dreams. They are
nostalgic and don't upset me. On the contrary, sometimes when
I lie down to go to sleep I "order" certain dreams.

There we are walking around Riga, the three of us – Misha,
Bulochka in his pram and me... The pram was from Yugoslavia.
Misha brought it when Gera was born... I'm dressed like the
Snow Maiden: white boots and a white fur coat. Misha brought
them, too. We walk and passers-by turn their heads – I hear:
"Tal! Tal!" And Misha says to them: "This is my Saska and our
Goosenysh, our Bulochka!"

I pack the suitcase for Misha's next journey and place a
note inside that says: "Bring shoes of size X and a suit of size
Y for MISHA. Mishanka! You only have one suit!" And then I
underline the message... Misha lifts up the suitcase and hums: *I
have told you not all the words.*

Ida is next to us. She's lying on her hospital bed under the portrait of Nekhemia Tal. She whispers to me: "My daughter, I beg you – don't forget Mishanka."

Joe is lying on another bed. He's regained consciousness: "Sallynka! Such good news! Misha came first in the blitz tourney!"

For some reason, Vasily Smyslov is also next to us: "See, you abandoned him and he turned to drink."

And Gera. He's carrying little Michelle (Miska!) in his arms. Gera says: "Mum! My, aren't you happy! See what wonderful people surround you!"

These and similar half-dreams, half-recollections visit me in various combinations. I wake up and it takes me a while to switch back into reality. And I think: who programmed Misha into my life? Who shot two arrows into us tied at the plumage by a hidden thread? Arrows that we can't extract. Or, if we can, then only together with our souls. And is there not some natural law explaining why Misha told me "not all the words"? After all, I didn't tell him "all the words" either... And anyway, people in love never manage to say "all the words" to each other in their lifetime. I suppose you can only say them *there*. There, where Misha is now.

The mystery of the phenomenon of Mikhail Tal has never been solved, and can never be fully solved, just like the mysteries of Michelangelo, Paganini and Cagliostro. For as long as the chess world exists, the bright, mysterious and magnetic star named Tal will sparkle above its horizon.
Baltiiskie Shakhmaty, 1992

Sometimes I recall an old and famous American film that I watched in my youth. In the Soviet Union, it was called *The*

Fate of a Soldier in America, but the American name for it was *The Roaring Twenties*. The hero is killed at the end of the film and he falls down some steps to the feet of a woman who had been with him his entire life. A policeman draws up and asks her: "How were you hooked up with him?" And the woman, as though recalling all their times together, replies: "I can never figure it out."

If somebody were to ask me the same question, I would give almost the same answer: "I can never figure it out... He was just *my Tal...*"

A Historical Note

As of the date of type-setting of this English translation (March 2019) Sally continues to live in Antwerp, aged 80. Gera lives in Beersheba and works as a dentist. He has two granddaughters. Sally's mother emigrated to Israel in 1990 together with Gera. She died in 2004. Her sister, Sally's Aunt Riva, lives in Israel and is aged 93. Opinions expressed by the people mentioned in this book were correct as of 1998, the date of the first Russian edition. Not all opinions are necessarily valid as of 2019.

Gera and me at the Monument to Mikhail Tal, Riga

CPSIA information can be obtained
at www.ICGtesting.com
Printed in the USA
LVHW080241040620
657364LV00009B/267

9 785604 176962